GUIDE TO
Making Time To Write

100+ TIME & PRODUCTIVITY MANAGEMENT TIPS
FOR TEXTBOOK AND ACADEMIC AUTHORS

Published by TAA — Textbook & Academic Authors Association

Guide to Making Time To Write: 100+ Time & Productivity Management Tips for Textbook and Academic Authors
Copyright © 2020 by Textbook & Academic Authors Association (TAA)

For further information contact:

Textbook & Academic Authors Association (TAA)
PO Box 367, Fountain City, WI 54629. Phone: (727) 563-0020 Email: Info@TAAonline.net Website: TAAonline.net

The information and advice in this book are accurate and effective to the best of our knowledge but are offered without guarantee. The contributors and Textbook & Academic Authors Association disclaim all liability in connection with the use of this book.

Publisher: Textbook & Academic Authors Association (TAA)
Project Manager: Kim Pawlak, Director of Publishing & Operations, TAA
Editors: Kim Pawlak, Director of Publishing & Operations, TAA; Eric Schmieder, Membership Marketing Manager, TAA
Cover and Interior Design/Composition: Tammy Seidick Graphic Design

ISBN 978-0-9975004-5-5

Publisher's Cataloging-In-Publication Data
(Prepared by The Donohue Group, Inc.)

Names: Pawlak, Kim, editor. | Schmieder, Eric J., editor.
Title: Guide to making time to write : 100+ time & productivity management tips for textbook and academic authors / [editors: Kim Pawlak, Director of Publishing & Operations, TAA [and] Eric Schmieder, Membership Marketing Manager, TAA].
Description: Fountain City, WI : Textbook & Academic Authors Association, [2020]
Identifiers: ISBN 9780997500455 | ISBN 9780997500462 (ebook)
Subjects: LCSH: Textbooks--Authorship--Handbooks, manuals, etc. | Academic writing--Handbooks, manuals, etc. | Time management--Handbooks, manuals, etc.
Classification: LCC LB3045.5 .G85 2020 (print) | LCC LB3045.5 (ebook) | DDC 371.3/2--dc23

The Textbook & Academic Authors Association (TAA) provides professional development resources, events, and networking opportunities for textbook authors and authors of scholarly journal articles and books. TAA's mission is to support textbook and academic authors in the creation of top-quality educational and scholarly works that stimulate the love of learning and foster the pursuit of knowledge. Its members are aspiring, new, and veteran textbook authors and authors of scholarly journal articles and books and come from a wide range of disciplines. Visit us at TAAonline.net.

Textbook & Academic
Authors Association

Table of Contents

Testimonials

"Looking to be more productive? Need more time to write? TAA's *Guide to Making Time to Write* is a treasure trove of guaranteed advice from the trenches that all of us can benefit from. Read it and amp up your output this week!" — John Bond, Publishing Consultant, RiverwindsConsulting.com

"As an academic writing coach, I work on time management with my clients a lot. The 128 tips offer something for every academic writer. What I appreciated the most, however, were the 25 software recommendations. Software is not my forte, so I was glad that the book devoted space to programs for me and my clients to try out." — Mary Beth Averill, PhD, an academic writing coach and editor, facilitates a weekly faculty writing group and works with individuals

"In addition to the book's many bulleted points you can pop like quick-fix pills, the sidebars of a 'Featured Strategy' bring warmth and relatability, with personal examples and photos of the writers/scholars advising how they specifically use time management and writing techniques." — Noelle Sterne, PhD, author of *Challenges in Writing Your Dissertation: Coping with the Emotional, Interpersonal, and Spiritual Struggles*

"*Guide to Making Time to Write: 100 + Time & Productivity Management Tips for Textbooks and Academic Authors* is a welcomed addition to my professional library. My only negative comment is that I needed it thirty years ago!" — Cliff Roberson, LLM, PhD. Author or co-author of over 50 textbooks, Professor Emeritus, Washburn University

"Supercharge your writing productivity with this practical and inspiring guide to making time to write. Learn from authors and me ntors and try out their advice—by experimenting with their tips you'll kickstart your personal writing process." — Bec Evans, author, writing productivity coach, Prolifiko

A Big Thanks to the Following Contributors

Mary Beth Averill, PhD, an academic writing coach and editor, facilitates a weekly faculty writing group and works with individuals
- Pay yourself first (Time Management, p. 24, #56)
- Celebrate your progress at every step (Time Management, p. 25, #58)
- Be present in case the muse decides to show up during your writing time (Time Management, p. 25, #59)
- Schedule time for intrusions (Time Management, p. 25, #60)
- Learn to say no, without guilt if possible (Time Management, p. 25, #61)
- Delegate—if you are used to handling emergencies, taking the lead on a paper, etc., realize that others can grow into this position with your support (Time Management, p. 25, #62)
- Be clear about your priorities (Time Management, p. 25, #63)
- Identify as a writer and a creative person (Productivity, p. 30, #76)
- Create multiple drafts starting with a zero draft (Productivity, p. 40, #116)
- Be willing to quit when, or even before, you reach diminishing returns (Productivity, p. 40, #117)
- Find a good metaphor to use to get you into your writing space (Productivity, p. 40, #118)
- Acknowledge author loneliness and find a way to mitigate it (Productivity, p. 41, #119)
- Make self-care a priority (Productivity, p. 41, #120)
- Edit last (Productivity, p. 41, #121)
- Enlist support of others with a visual reminder (Productivity, p. 41, #122)
- Make a list of short activities you can do when you feel too tired/busy/burned out to be creative (Productivity, p. 41, #123)
- Find an accountability partner (Productivity, p. 41, #124)
- Keep a writing journal to note your progress, where to start the next time you sit down to write, and as a place to note down things that could have interrupted you that you will tend to later (Productivity, p. 42, #125)

Teresa Bell, Associate Professor of German and Second Language Acquisition
- Set aside time every day (at least Monday-Friday) to write (Time Management, p. 18, #30)
- Have sticky notes available for when thoughts come to mind that aren't related to writing (Time Management, p. 18, #31)

Kenneth Campbell, Specialist in the history of the British Isles and a recipient of Monmouth's Distinguished Teacher Award
- Prioritize your writing tasks within your schedule (Time Management, p. 18, #32)

Gladys Childs, Dean of Freshman Success, author of articles and the forthcoming *Logic Made Easy*, published by Cognella
- Set-up your course schedule each semester so you can have days where you do not teach or have regularly scheduled meetings (Time Management, p. 12, #5)
- Use the Pomodoro Technique (Time Management, p. 12, #6)

William Suhs Cleveland, Professor of Nonprofit Management
- Write every day, even if it is short as 15-30 minutes (Time Management, p. 11, #3)
- Develop a full pipeline of projects that allow you to keep a couple of different ideas going at the same time (Time Management, p. 24, #53)
- Have an accountability partner that you share your progress with (Productivity, p. 39, #108)

Jeff Conte, Ph.D., author of *Work in the 21st Century: An Introduction to Industrial and Organizational Psychology* (6e, Wiley)
- Right after finishing updates and revisions on a new edition of my textbook, I start an electronic file that includes the detailed table of contents from that recently published edition (Productivity, p. 30, #77)

Lisa Daniels, Professor of Economics and International Studies, Washington College
- Set a weekly time goal divided into daily doses based on other obligations (Time Management, p. 15, #17)
- Start a writing group (Time Management, p. 19, #38)
- Writing Group Template (Time Management & Productivity Templates, p. 47)

Dr. Derrick C. Darden, Professor of Human Management, Tiffin University
- Break down your projects into bite-size pieces (Productivity, p. 38, #103)

Rose Ernst, PhD, Academic Editor & Consultant
- Tackle daily overwhelm using "decision decoupling" and "emotional decoupling" (Productivity, p. 27, #69)

Bec Evans, author, writing productivity coach, Prolifiko
- Can't write now? Test your assumption (Time Management, p. 25, #64)
- Prioritize writing in your life using the "rocks and pebbles" method (Time Management, p. 26, #65)
- Find time to write using the "traffic light" approach (Time Management, p. 26, #66)

Dr. Kathy B. Ewoldt, Assistant Professor of Special Education, University of Texas at San Antonio
- Bi-Weekly Writing Tracking Tool (Time Management & Productivity Templates, p. 44)

Domenica Favero, Associate Professor of Psychological Science, author of *Introduction to Theories of Personality*
- Set a timer just to get you started (Time Management, p. 17, #25)

Dr. Óscar Fernández, Diversity, Equity, and Inclusion Coordinator, University Studies, Portland State University
- Resist the greatest enemy of writing in higher education: Email. (Productivity, p. 37, #99)

Gertrude J. Fraser, Associate Professor of Anthropology, University of Virginia, author of *African American Midwifery in the South: Dialogues of Birth, Race, and Memory* and several articles about diversity and inclusion in academia
- Play with words and allow your mind to be distracted—is there a memory, an image, an overheard conversation? Take time to write them down in a voice that perhaps you would not use in an academic article, or pretend to be writing for your grandmother who spoke a different language (Time Management, p. 21, #41)

Joseph Godlewski, Assistant Professor of Architecture, author of *Introduction to Architecture: Global Disciplinary Knowledge*
- Take advantage of "thinking time" (Productivity, p. 39, #106)
- Capture ideas while on the go using your iPhone Notes app (Productivity, p. 39, #107)

Beth L. Hewett, PhD., President and Executive Coach, Defend & Publish, LLC, academic coaches for adult writers. Author of numerous books and articles
- Look at your collaboration efforts with co-authors and/or co-editors as a series of activities for which each person might volunteer or be assigned (Productivity, p. 42, #126)
- Utilize cloud-based software like Google Docs, which allows multiple authors to work simultaneously on collaborative projects (Productivity, p. 42, #127)
- Collaborative Writing Log (Time Management & Productivity Templates, p. 49)

Lilian H. Hill, Professor of Adult Education, editor of *Assessment, Evaluation, and Accountability in Adult Education*
- Practice your writing regularly (Productivity, p. 32, #80)

Mariëlle Hoefnagels, Professor of Biology and Microbiology/Plant Biology, University of Oklahoma, author of *Biology: Concepts and Investigations* and *Biology: The Essentials*, both published by McGraw-Hill
- Keep a detailed timesheet (Time Management, p. 16, #21)

Ahmed Ibrahim, PhD, Sr. Education Research Consultant, Johns Hopkins University
- Use a dedicated screen to show only 2 things: a timeline of project progress and writing time tracking (Productivity, p. 28, #71)

Ella L. Ingram, Associate Dean for Professional Development and Professor of Biology, Rose-Hulman Institute of Technology
- Backwards Planning Worksheet (Time Management & Productivity Templates, p. 50-51)

Burcu Izci, Assistant Professor, Early Childhood Education
- Monthly Goal Setting Worksheet (Time Management & Productivity Templates, p. 45)

Dr. Jane Jones, Academic Editor and Consultant, Up In Consulting
- Find opportunities throughout the day to do something (Time Management, p. 23, #51)
- Create a variety of goals, both in time (daily, weekly, and monthly) and importance (deadlines, passion-based, external pressure, time needed, and long-term importance) (Time Management, p. 23, #52)
- Determine what is important and get it done first (Time Management, p. 24, #54)
- Create systems of accountability (Time Management, p. 24, #55)

Dana C. Kemery, Associate Professor, College of Nursing and Health Professions, Drexel University
- Have a strategy, or a few strategies, other than a specific space that signals you to write (Productivity, p. 28, #70)

Mike Kennamer, community college dean and academic and textbook author
- Use a project status board as a tool for monitoring the status of projects (Time Management, p. 22, #47)

Kathleen P. King has published more than 32 books including *147 Practical Tips for Emerging Scholars* and *The Professor's Guide to Taming Technology*
- Make lists, schedules and charts, and always track your progress (Time Management, p. 16, #18)
- Make writing appointments with yourself (Time Management, p. 16, #19)
- Be mindful that time and location matter (Time Management, p. 16, #20)
- Turn off notifications on your computer and phone (Productivity, p. 39, #109)

- Take breaks (Productivity, p. 39, #110)
- Do not ignore ergonomics (Productivity, p. 39, #111)
- Use writing accelerators (Productivity, p. 39, #112)
- Keep a virtual filing cabinet (Productivity, p. 39, #113)
- Save online material as a PDF (Productivity, p. 39, #114)
- Utilize a reference control system (Productivity, p. 40, #115)

Anna Kowalcze-Pawlik, Ph.D., University of Lodz
- Use a whiteboard to track your projects (Time Management, p. 14, #11)
- Plan ahead, splitting your workload into manageable wholes (Productivity, p. 27, #68)

Konnie Kustron, Professor, Eastern Michigan University, and co-author of *Case Studies on Women in Business* (2e)
- Use the "Brainstorm Writing" technique (Productivity, p. 29, #74)

Robert (Bob) W. Lucas, author of the 2019 McGuffey Longevity Award winner, *Customer Service Skills for Success*, 7e
- Maintain an "idea folder" (Time Management, p. 17, #27)
- Start your book project with a rough outline (Time Management, p. 17, #28)
- Use your circadian rhythm (your internal 24-hour clock) to find your daily primetime and match it with your life schedule to determine the best time for you to write (Time Management, p. 18, #29)
- Continually gather new ideas and content (Productivity, p. 36, #93)
- Determine your purpose for writing (Productivity, p. 36, #97)
- Become knowledgeable about the textbook authoring and publishing process (Productivity, p. 37, #98)

Chin-Nu Lin, Professor of Nursing, author of several nursing scholarly articles
- Set up and prioritize goals for most days (Time Management, p. 17, #23)
- Use your smartphone calendar to track your goals (Time Management, p. 17, #24)
- Make time for yourself (Productivity, p. 36, #92)
- Weekly Time Tracking Calendar (Time Management & Productivity Templates, p. 48)

Guy Marriage, author of the 2020 Most Promising New Textbook Award winner, *Tall: the Design and Construction of High-Rise Architecture*, 1e
- Write (Productivity, p. 37, #101)

Meggin McIntosh, The PhD of Productivity®, Coach, Teacher, Author
- Divide your writing project into "hunks, chunks, and bites" (Time Management, p. 20, #40)

Erin McTigue, Academic Coach, The Positive Academic
- Harness the power of habits for writing productivity (Productivity, p. 32, #81)

Felicia Moore Mensah, Professor of Science Education, The Scholar Mentor, Academic Coach
- Set dates on your calendar as appointments for writing (Time Management, p. 19, #37)

Karen Morris, Distinguished Professor of Law, author of twelve textbooks, a magazine column, trade books, and a publisher's blog
- Create an organizational system (Productivity, p. 29, #73)

Richard Mullins, Professor of Chemistry, aspiring author of a 1st edition organic chemistry book
- Develop a writing streak (Productivity, p. 42, #128)

Dr. Diana Newport-Peace, Postdoctoral Research Fellow and freelance consultant in academic strategy
- Allow yourself to prioritize your research and writing over helping others (Time Management, p. 22, #45)
- Commit to writing for 25 minutes without distractions at least once per day (commonly referred to as the Pomodoro Method) (Time Management, p. 22, #46)

Shawn E. Nordell, PhD., author of the 2014 Most Promising New Textbook, *Animal Behavior*, currently in its 3rd edition
- Find yourself an "effort buddy" who can send you a virtual trophy or thumbs up every time you get in your daily writing time (Time Management, p. 22, #44)

Dr. Noreen B. Oeding, Assistant Nursing Professor
- Use the "Rule of 5's" to help you develop concepts, establish writing in the limited time you have, and produce work that is publication and presentation worthy (Productivity, p. 31, #78)

Daniel Pardo, Assistant Professor of Flute, Prairie View A&M University, Yamaha Performing Artist & Clinician
- Trigger imagination and awaken all senses by going out for "Beethoven's Walks" (Productivity, p. 35, #88)
- Use voice memo on your phone to make lists of writing topics (Productivity, p. 35, #89)
- Go to bed early and wake up at 3 or 4 a.m. to write (Productivity, p. 35, #90)
- Give yourself quick deadlines to meet within the hour (Productivity, p. 35, #91)

Kevin Patton, author of award-winning textbooks and manuals in human anatomy and physiology
- When working at home around family members (and pets), consider including them rather than pushing them away as you write (Productivity, p. 34, #87)

Katy Peplin, Coach, Editor, and Community Builder, Thrive PhD
- Use defensive scheduling to protect your time rather than filling it up (Time Management, p. 15, #16)

Elsa Peterson, freelance developmental editor and writer with more than 30 years of experience
- Determine the amount of time and time of day/night when you need to write (Time Management, p. 20, #39)

Jamie Pope, co-author of the 2020 Textbook Excellence Award winner, *Nutrition for a Changing World*, 2e
- Develop established deadlines (Time Management, p. 15, #13)
- Try to focus on one chapter or "assignment" at a time, completing that as much as possible (Productivity, p. 34, #82)

Thrishika Potan, CIE graduate student at Loyola Academy, author of published nutrition-based journal article, writer and content creator
- Make sure that no matter how hard it is, you've made a step towards your "true to yourself" goals every day (Productivity, p. 37, #100)

Dr. Margaret Puskar-Pasewicz, academic editor, indexer, and writing coach
- Use a writing journal to jot down ideas and goals or do some freewriting (Time Management, p. 13, #7)

Cliff Roberson, LLM, PhD., author or co-author of over 50 textbooks, Professor Emeritus, Washburn University
- Write at least 3 pages a day (Time Management, p. 17, #26)

Susan Robison, Psychologist and Faculty Development Consultant, Professor DeStressor, author, *The Peak Performing Professor: A Practical Guide to Productivity and Happiness*
- Prioritize which tasks are worthy of your resources of time, talent, energy, and attention (Productivity, p. 36, #96)

Kathryn Roulston, Professor of Qualitative Research, author, editor and co-author of three books and author and co-author of over 70 articles and book chapters
- Have a goal of writing five days a week, and routinely log your research and writing time (Time Management, p. 14, #10)

Joanna Salapska-Gelleri, Associate Professor of Cognitive Psychology, Florida Gulf Coast University, and co-author of *Mind, Brain, and Artificial Intelligence*
- When working with coauthors, be respectful of each other's time commitments when enforcing deadlines (Time Management, p. 15, #14)
- Create a system that allows you and your coauthor to write together that holds both of you accountable and keeps you on schedule (Time Management, p. 15, #15)
- Have a specific, but flexible, project plan (Productivity, p. 27, #67)

Timothy F. Slater, Endowed Professor of Science Education, author of 24 books, 130 scholarly journal articles, and the academic time management book, *The Busy Professor*
- Use the Door Hanger Barrier (Productivity, p. 30, #75)

Kirk St. Amant, Professor and Eunice C. Williamson Endowed Chair in Technical Communication, Louisiana Tech University and Director of Tech's Center for Health Communication (CHC)
- Use the "focused-early-dedicated-done" (FEDD) time management strategy (Time Management, p. 11, #1)
- Use a timer (Time Management, p. 11, #2)

Noelle Sterne, PhD, dissertation and mainstream writing coach and editor and author of *Challenges in Writing Your Dissertation: Coping with the Emotional, Interpersonal, and Spiritual Struggles*
- Track your activities with a time log (Time Management, p. 11, #4)
- Count time instead of words (Time Management, p. 14, #9)

Dannelle D. Stevens, Professor, Faculty-in-Residence for Academic Writing, Portland State University, book author, experienced academic writing and career coach
- Use the three verbs—listing, counting, graphing—as important actions in developing a powerful, predictable, productive, and personal writing practice (Time Management, p. 13, #8)
- Think of time management more as time allocation than time management (Time Management, p. 18, #34)
- Use the word "practice" as a noun as in "developing a writing practice" or a verb, "practice my writing" (Time Management, p. 18, #35)

Robert B. Tallitsch, textbook and academic author, Professor Emeritus and Writer in Residence, Dept. of Biology, Augustana College (Illinois)
- Aim for (but be flexible) for an end-of-the-day goal(s) for the amount of content to be written (Time Management, p. 15, #12)
- Use a hard copy calendar to create a queue for writing tasks (Time Management, p. 16, #22)
- If you are having difficulty writing, be flexible (Productivity, p. 34, #83)
- Dress for work if you write at home (Productivity, p. 34, #84)

- When it comes to proofreading, make a check-off list so that you cover each and every task in the proper order for each and every page that needs to be proofread (Productivity p. 34, #85)
- Use multiple monitors when writing (Productivity, p. 34, #86)

Mitali Thakor, Assistant Professor of Science in Society, Wesleyan University
- Write for 20 minutes (freehand or typing) as the first thing you do upon waking up (Productivity, p. 36, #94)
- Change up how you write (Productivity, p. 36, #95)

Christine Tulley, Professor of English, author of *How Writing Faculty Write*, and Coach, Defend & Publish, LLC
- Develop a writing project management chart to track all writing projects that need attention (Time Management, p. 23, #50)
- Scholarship Tracking Chart (Time Management & Productivity Templates, p. 49)

Dr. Niti D. Villinger, Former Associate Professor of Management, Hawaii Pacific University, author of various articles and book length manuscripts
- Develop a daily writing habit by finding quiet times during the day to engage in writing (Time Management, p. 18, #33)
- Be inspired by current events (Productivity, p. 37, #102)
- Keep learning (Productivity, p. 38, #104)
- Enlist the help of a writing buddy at home or at your place of work (Productivity, p. 38, #105)

Dale Walker, DBA, CPA (inactive), US Navy Veteran 1962-1968, author of *Constitution to Crisis* (2015)
- Find a quiet, comfortable place to work (Productivity, p. 28, #72)

Phil Wankat, happily retired professor & author
- Find time throughout your day where you can carve out writing time (Time Management, p. 19, #36)

William H. Weare, Jr., Director of Public Services, Evans Library, Texas A&M University
- Get your goals down on paper and prioritize them (Time Management, p. 23, #48)
- Overcome negative thinking (Time Management, p. 23, #49)

Wendi K. Zimmer, Professor of Writing and Communication
- Color Me Productive (Time Management, p. 24, #57)
- Keep both a writing and productivity log to help you not only plan your writing time but also keep track of where you are in your writing and what you need to do next (Productivity, p. 32, #79)
- Academic Writing Checklist (Time Management & Productivity Templates, p. 46)

Software Recommendations Contributed By:

- **Teresa Bell**, Associate Professor of German and Second Language Acquisition
- **Gladys Childs**, Dean of Freshman Success, author of articles and the forthcoming *Logic Made Easy*, published by Cognella
- **Lisa Daniels**, Professor of Economics and International Studies, Washington College
- **Domenica Favero**, Associate Professor of Psychological Science, author of *Introduction to Theories of Personality*
- **Dr. Óscar Fernández**, Diversity, Equity, and Inclusion Coordinator, University Studies, Portland State University
- **Dallas Glenn**, freelance academic author, writer, editor, and proofreader
- **Ahmed Ibrahim, PhD**, Sr. Education Research Consultant, Johns Hopkins University
- **Burcu Izci**, Assistant Professor, Early Childhood Education
- **Katya Jordan**, Assistant Professor of Russian
- **Dana C. Kemery**, Associate Professor, College of Nursing and Health Professions, Drexel University
- **Mike Kennamer**, community college dean and academic and textbook author
- **Kathleen P. King** has published more than 32 books including *147 Practical Tips for Emerging Scholars* and *The Professor's Guide to Taming Technology*
- **Kevin Patton**, author of award-winning textbooks and manuals in human anatomy and physiology
- **Thrishika Potan**, CIE graduate student at Loyola Academy, author of published nutrition-based journal article, writer and content creator
- **Margaret Puskar-Pasewicz**, academic editor, indexer, and writing coach
- **Joanna Salapska-Gelleri**, Associate Professor of Cognitive Psychology, Florida Gulf Coast University, and co-author of *Mind, Brain, and Artificial Intelligence*
- **Eric Schmieder**, textbook author and college faculty member, computer technology discipline
- **Christine Tulley**, Professor of English, author of *How Writing Faculty Write*, and Defend and Publish Coach
- **Tracy Tuten**, author of *Principles of Marketing for a Digital Age*

Introduction

You know you should be writing at least 15 minutes a day. But with all the demands on your time, how can you find 15 minutes or more to spare? And when you do find the time to write, it's often hard to break free of the distractions and build momentum in the time that you have. We get it. Making time to write—and doing it productively—can be challenging.

So, to help you succeed, we've collected 100+ successful tips and strategies—and a lot of inspiration—from authors who have made the time and made it work. In this *Guide to Making Time to Write*, you will find just what you need to boost your productivity, adjust your routine, and focus on your writing efforts once and for all. Isn't it time for you to make the time to write?

Time Management

1 **Use the "focused-early-dedicated-done" (FEDD) time management strategy.** The FEDD approach can help identify activities to split into tasks and schedule one morning each day to complete parts of that overall activity.

- **Focus:** Make the first thing you do the task requiring the greatest focus—not necessarily the most pressing, but the one requiring singular attention.

- **Early:** Rise 60-90 minutes before your conventional workday "waking time" to create a cushion before the pressures to dive into "work" mode distractions.

- **Dedicated:** Dedicate all "early" time to working only on the task requiring attention, nothing else, until the full time is up.

- **Done:** Allow only those "early" minutes to work on the task to reduce temptations to shift focus or delay actions. If you need more than these morning minutes, you likely aren't dealing with "one task", but a series of activities that each needs focused attention.

2 **Use a timer.** Set it for 60-90 minutes with "reminders" identifying when you have 60, 30, 15, and 5 minutes left to focus on completing a task.

3 **Write every day, even if it is as short as 15-30 minutes.** For days you don't want to do much or are very busy, prioritize tasks so you have a short task waiting for you on that day. For instance, you might think "this paragraph is really rough, and I need to spend 20 minutes revising it." Set aside time on Saturday morning with only that paragraph as the focus.

4 **Track your activities with a time log.** You don't need to keep it forever, but keeping it for a week or two, or a month, will show you how you're using your time. You can experiment, reallocate your time (alternate mornings and evenings, or weekdays and weekends, depending on your other obligations), establish patterns that really feel good, have revelations, or make other surprising discoveries, and learn to use your time in different ways. With a time log, you'll give yourself more credit for using time rightly and forgive yourself for wasting time. When you make conscious choices, you'll feel more in charge of your time and will recognize that you actually have more time than you imagined. And as you desire and feel impelled, you'll choose more of your time for your writing.

If you're an academic with students and also a writer, try writing in the mornings and addressing student work, emails, and calls in the afternoons and evenings. A professor shares her time log:

TIME	ACTIVITY
6:30 am	Rise (a good day).
6:33 - 7:15 am	Shower, dress, check TV guide, record 42 shows I'll never watch.
7:15 - 8:15 am	Read, meditate, plan day with (ideal) time allocations.
8:15 - 8:45 am	Breakfast, talk with hubby (that is, listen to him talk).
8:45 - 10:00 am	Scan Internet news (gossip), check client emails, answer a few, wipe kitchen counter, take out something to defrost for dinner.
10:00 - 11:15 am	Work on novel (finally!).
11:15 - 11:30 am	Browse in a magazine (needed break).
11:30 am - 12:30 pm	Attack current student's dissertation.
12:30 - 1:15 pm	Lunch . . . then nap . . . .

Reviewing the time log, she not only blushed but recognized eight benefits of using one:

- Identify the activities most important to you.
- Identify your pattern and where you can improve.
- Make more conscious choices.
- See how many things you've really accomplished.
- Give yourself permission and freedom to relax into the specific activity.
- Build in needed and non-guilt-making breaks.
- Strengthen your resolve to do better or keep up the good pattern and go further.
- Gain a great sense of control over your time and see how you can make time choices to inch closer to, and reach, your writing goals.

5 **Set-up your course schedule each semester so you can have days where you do not teach or have regularly scheduled meetings.** Block these days off so no one can schedule meetings. If this is hard to do, then talk to your department chair or dean and ask to have one day a week where you can focus solely on your writing, perhaps a Monday or Friday.

6 **Use the Pomodoro Technique.** This was originally developed by Francesco Cirillo. With this technique, you break your time down into intervals (25, 30, or 45 minutes) where you write and then take a short break to refresh yourself. After every four working intervals, take a longer break.

7 **Use a writing journal to jot down ideas and goals or do some freewriting.** Your writing journal can be as formal or informal as you like, but the main point is to keep it simple and not create another onerous task for yourself. One of the best ways to use a writing journal is to reflect at the end of a writing session on what you've accomplished and where you want to start next time. Then, at the beginning of your next session, you don't have to waste time reviewing what you've already done and figuring out where to start.

8 **Use the three verbs—listing, counting, graphing—as important actions in developing a powerful, predictable, productive, and personal writing practice.**

"First of all, I list my daily goals on a sheet that I check at the beginning and end of my writing sessions. This helps me learn about writing goals that can be done in a given time frame and is a visual and reinforcing checklist of the things I have accomplished.

Second, besides listing, I have also counted and graphed words at the same time. Sometimes I set a daily goal of 400 words. In Microsoft Word, go to the pulldown menu 'Tools', and you will see 'Word Count'. This is the current word count across the whole manuscript. If you want to just count a section, highlight that section and pulldown Tools again to Word Count and that number will be the words in the section highlighted. This is handy when you only want to count manuscript words, not including the references. Before writing, I note the number of words in the manuscript. After writing, I check the number of words. The difference, of course, is the number of words I have generated in the session. When I am trying to generate text at the beginning of a project, I make a bar graph for each day that has the number of words written. It is really reinforcing to see that bar graph filled in for every day. This method is not for everyone and it does not work when you are at the editing phase because you are probably subtracting words rather than adding them.

Third, counting and graphing again, but this time I count and graph time spent writing. This record helps me make sure I have actually spent a decent amount of time on my project. In addition, it is a reality check for the weeks when I think I have written a lot and, yet, well, actually I did not spend as much time as I thought. So, I can readjust my priorities in the next week."

— **Dannelle D. Stevens, Professor, Faculty-in-Residence for Academic Writing, Portland State University, book author, experienced academic writing and career coach**

9 **Count time instead of words.** Tracking time rather than words can free you from your inner "word count critic". Record your time stints. Use a simple graph with five columns in Word (Excel works too): the day, date, time from-to, number or fraction of devoted hours, and project or title name. Keep your graph by the month, and it will help you see (a) the times of day you've written, (b) the better days and times, and (c) your sustained efforts on various projects.

Some benefits of the time count method:

- You relax into the session. Start the session with an affirmation: "I deserve." No frenzied typing simply to fill the page or meet the word count.

- The time goal means that you take your time. You sink into the work. You immerse.

- As you immerse, you realize you may need information, so you do research.

- You incorporate the information you found. Write yourself notes in the draft, "more here?" In the next draft, you can edit, synopsize, expand.

- Without the word count constraint, you engage with what you've just learned.

- If your current project doesn't require research, and you find the words don't come, you have the freedom to get quiet, connect with your Inner Writer, and ask: "What is my next step, my next word?" Don't hurry or fret. The answers will come.

- Your answers may surface not for the section you're in but as thoughts for the next segment, section, chapter, or even book. Take these thoughts down! Place or file them in the most logical place, where you'll remember or come across them later.

- Your fingers don't have to be busy every second to meet some impossible word count to match or beat another writer's. As you give yourself freedom, you may find, to your delight, that after a few minutes the words start to flow.

- The most convincing reason for tracking minutes over words is satisfaction. With a hovering word quota, you can be tempted to type anything. When you do, you may leave the session with an unfulfilled, empty feeling, a feeling that you haven't really done anything. But with your time count, you've produced at least part of a decent draft, to your great and grateful satisfaction.

10 **Have a goal of writing five days a week, and routinely log your research and writing time.** The log should include time spent reading, writing, and editing, as well as team meetings when involved in team projects. By writing daily and logging your time you will be better able to prioritize writing and complete writing tasks in a timely way.

11 **Use a whiteboard to track your projects.** Visualization of your workplan is the key. If you find out that time management software does not work for you, go analog, create your workplan and stick to it, rewarding yourself once the tasks are done.

12 **Aim for (but be flexible) for an end-of-the-day goal(s) for the amount of content to be written.** Be flexible because you may not make that goal for a variety of reasons but be FIXED in that you do not want to add another goal at the end of the day if you have met your goal(s) of the day. Reward yourself by taking time off.

13 **Develop established deadlines.** Having established deadlines helps keep you on track—knowing that your work and timeliness impacts others and helps keep the project on track and on time.

14 **When working with coauthors, be respectful of each other's time commitments when enforcing deadlines.** The early phases of a collaboration will bring out the best and least good sides of your team's cooperative skills, but time should help you get to know each other better. Understanding the diversity of personalities and writing paths of your coauthor(s) can help a team be more accepting and less annoyed with the other individual, especially as you get to know each other's strengths and quirks. If you expect a bit of tension, then you can work past it and model a healthy "diffusion" behavior, rather than buy into the negative vibe that might be spreading from the other contributors. A way to get to know each other is to schedule some virtual face-to-face time. Voice-only conference calls lose a lot in the translation as you don't get to see each others' body language and awkward pauses brew discomfort. Seeing one another face-to-face also helps those whose conversational styles are more shy and difficult to interpret. These meetings don't have to revolve around heavy planning, they can just relate to a few agenda items and some discussion of what's going well or what is challenging.

15 **Create a system that allows you and your coauthor to write together that holds both of you accountable and keeps you on schedule.** Hold regular meetings to discuss progress and make real-time notes in a shared document as you talk. Assign topics with your initials and make notes about how arguments need to progress or what else you need to flesh out or do deeper research on.

16 **Use defensive scheduling to protect your time rather than filling it up.** There are two kinds of scheduling—appointment and defensive. Appointment scheduling is pretty self-explanatory—you have somewhere to be at a certain time, and so you put it in your calendar. These are the kinds of things that people usually use their calendar/schedule/planner for, and of course, it's useful. It gets you to where you need to be when you need to be there! But defensive scheduling is a little different. It's about protecting time, rather than filling it up. You put something on your calendar so you WON'T give that time away to someone/something else. You claim your time before someone else does.

17 **Set a weekly time goal divided into daily doses based on other obligations.** Instead of setting pages or chapters per week as a goal, create a weekly time goal and then divide that into the five workdays based on other commitments for each day. For example, commit to 9 hours a week overall with 3 hours per day on two non-teaching days and 1 hour per day on the three teaching days. Then record your progress each day on a spreadsheet including the time spent writing and what you worked on. By working on a project every day, you always know exactly where to start and hit the ground running. By keeping track of the time each day, you are motivated to get it done early and might even get ahead. Working longer than the set goal on one day means you can use the extra time later in the week for other projects or just to relax!

18 **Make lists, schedules and charts, and always track your progress.** They give you freedom, they give you control. But they're never meant to choke you. Creating lists and schedules along with tracking your progress are ways to aid you in staying on track and to motivate you to get the work done.

19 **Make writing appointments with yourself.** Treat your writing time as sacred time; nothing else should be scheduled during this time. Treat this appointment with your writing like you would any other appointment—you show up.

20 **Be mindful that time and location matter.** To be most effective you need to understand what time and location work best for you. If you are most productive writing in the morning, that's when you schedule your writing time. Write in a location that you are comfortable in and that is free of distractions. This will allow you to be the most productive.

21 **Keep a detailed timesheet.** Every time you sit down to write, keep track of the time you spend on each book, article, or other project. Create a spreadsheet for each project, with a tab for each month. Just keeping track of the total amount of time you devote to writing provides useful insights into your overall time management, but the real power is in the details. If you divide your spreadsheet columns into categories, you can paint a rich portrait of where your writing time is going. Each author must decide which categories are most useful. A textbook author, for example, might have separate columns for first draft, photo selections, art revisions, copyedited manuscript, first pass pages, revised pages, and miscellaneous. The beauty of this system is that when the next edition comes along, you will already know that, say, corrections to first pass pages require an average of 5 hours per chapter. For a book with 40 chapters, you'll need to set aside about 200 hours, just for that stage. That's a big chunk of time! Throughout the craziness of writing and production, your timesheets from previous projects will provide the objective data you need to manage your time.

Featured Strategy

22 **Use a hard copy calendar to create a queue for writing tasks.** "I use a generic calendar where you enter days of the year. I add new tasks (from my coauthor or editor or whomever) to the BOTTOM of the queue so I stay on task with my daily goals. I work up the queue—I DO NOT skip around. For 'time sensitive requests' I notify the sender that I will get to it as soon as my tasks for that day are completed. At the start of any project I always ask that my editor/coauthor/whomever is understanding and clear on this. (This is especially important so that I don't lose my train of thought, be it a productive or unproductive day). In addition to my hard copy 'to do' list I duplicate that electronically with the app 'Reminders' (I am a Mac user) and I keep that on my main computer screen (I use three screens attached to my desktop computer)."

— Robert B. Tallitsch, textbook and academic author, Professor Emeritus and Writer in Residence, Dept. of Biology, Augustana College (Illinois)

23 **Set up and prioritize goals for most days.** A to-do-list is helpful, but don't feel stressed if you aren't able to achieve all of the goals you set every time. Allow yourself to be flexible and to prepare for unpredictable situations that arise.

24 **Use your smartphone calendar to track your goals.** The calendar feature in most smartphones allow for entering basic information such as event, date, time and location, and to set up reminders. Synchronizing the calendar features from different devices (desktop computer, laptop, tablet and cellphone) could help you to consolidate your schedules into one place.

25 **Set a timer just to get you started.** Setting a timer and writing for a specific amount of time puts you in the flow of writing and you'll often find you will continue to write beyond the time you set. Knowing that you only have to produce for a certain amount of time reduces the pressure to write and makes it easier to start.

26 **Write at least 3 pages a day.** Don't worry about spelling or the proper words during the first draft. It will only be seen by the waste basket.

27 **Maintain an "idea folder".** This can be in the form of a file cabinet or an e-file system. You can use this idea folder to capture potential book topics that come to mind, working titles, a rough draft of chapter titles or topics, and whatever else comes to mind about your project. By creating a tangible list, you can revisit the concepts when you have time to start writing the book. Since these ideas might come to you as you're walking, sitting in a parking lot, or walking around a store, you can also use your cell phone to quickly record your thoughts or send yourself an email to add to your idea file when you get back to your office.

28 **Start your book project with a rough outline.** Just as you wouldn't get into your car and say "Let's take a road trip" without first looking at a map or doing some research, you shouldn't waste time aimlessly trying to come up with book ideas as you write. Before starting a book project, always start with a rough outline. This may change several times as you work through text creation. As you develop the outline, choose a working title and subtitle along with 10-12 tentative chapter titles. Under each chapter, draft out ideas of what content might fit into it. You can also use a bulleted list of potential chapter concepts or elements or use a paragraph approach and write 1-2 sections of what you plan for the chapter.

29 **Use your circadian rhythm (your internal 24-hour clock) to find your daily primetime and match it with your life schedule to determine the best time for you to write.** Some people are at their best in the morning while others hit their peak later in the day. Once you identify the best time for you to write, put it on your daily calendar and try to stick to the schedule. If you do not take a planned approach, you will likely find yourself procrastinating. You may also encounter the dreaded writer's block syndrome. When that occurs, you will find yourself sitting unmotivated and staring at a blank computer screen or piece of paper.

30 **Set aside time every day (at least Monday-Friday) to write.** Make sure the time set aside for writing is never interrupted. Turn off all notifications, including cell phones.

31 **Have sticky notes available for when thoughts come to mind that aren't related to writing.** Write down the thoughts (take the dog for a walk, water the garden, take chicken out of the freezer to thaw for dinner, etc.) on the sticky notes, then forget about them until writing time is over.

32 **Prioritize your writing tasks within your schedule.** The only way to have time for something is to make time for something.

- Break complex tasks into smaller, manageable ones.
- Plan your schedule around your deadline.
- Take advantage of opportunities that allow you more time for writing.

33 **Develop a daily writing habit by finding quiet times during the day to engage in writing.** From the early morning hours before breakfast to lunch and coffee breaks, a writer must find the time to write, however scant they might be. Even if the ideas come to you like fleeting birds in a sky, you should jot them down in a small notepad and then develop the ideas in your mind for future writing goals. It is possible to encourage this "appetizer" of writing practice, before you actually invest in the "entrée" of written outcomes which will take more time. And the "dessert" is like the final meal course where you edit, refine and enjoy what you have written.

34 **Think of time management more as time allocation than time management.** The idea is that you are allocating time to certain projects rather than just managing your time. Allocation implies more agency in scheduling your projects and activities. You are choosing what to do and when to do it and that choice has implications for your life and your career.

35 **Use the word "practice" as a noun as in "developing a writing practice" or a verb, "practice my writing".** To have any practice from playing a musical instrument to running a 5K, you need to practice. Practice with feedback is the best for improving practice so that we can refine our practice to accomplish our goals. Look at all your time allocation strategies as opportunities to get feedback on what worked and what didn't. Do I get more done in the morning? How did I use my journal when working on a project? How did that work? What seemed to work best in handling this revise and resubmit? By reflecting on the tools and strategies you use in allocating time, setting goals and completing manuscripts, you will learn about what works for you as a writer. When you do, you will see that your writing practice improves. You will feel like you are more in control of your time and can guide improvement, so that you truly have an enjoyable and sustainable writing practice.

Featured Strategy

36 **Find time throughout your day where you can carve out writing time.** "When I was department head there was no time to write between 9 and 5; however, if there were no morning meetings I could write from whenever I got into the office (usually around 7:45 a.m.) until around 9:00 a.m. And every evening people would go home around 5:00 p.m. and I would have free time to write until 5:50 p.m. when I went home for dinner. May not sound like a lot of time, but I finished one textbook and wrote another during the eight years I was department head."

— Phil Wankat, happily retired professor & author

37 **Set dates on your calendar as appointments for writing.** The blocks of time set aside for writing and organizing documents can then be written into a writing log (in Google Docs) with dates, times, and goals.

38 **Start a writing group.** Create a shared Google Sheet with colleagues who are also working on writing projects. Have four columns for each member–Daily goal in minutes, Actual time spent writing, Own comments on your work, Others' comments on your work. Each row is a new day. Use it to comment on your own work and to give each other words of encouragement. Having colleagues review your goals and your ups and downs gives you a sense of community– you are not in this alone. Plus, it keeps you motivated.

Here's an example Google Sheet for a writing group (download this as a PDF at TAAonline.net/resources with password TIME20):

	Participant: LS				Participant: SD				Participant: SG			
Date	**Goal Minutes**	**Actual Minutes**	**Own Comments**	**Others' Comments**	**Goal Minutes**	**Actual Minutes**	**Own Comments**	**Others' Comments**	**Goal Minutes**	**Actual Minutes**	**Own Comments**	**Others' Comments**
Wed., Feb 12, 2020	35	28	I'm finding that even a few minutes a day keeps me on track. I don't lose as much time trying to figure out where to pick up again.	SG: I completely agree. Even a few minutes helps.		20	Does a Skype call with a co-author count?	LS: It sure does! I even count my minutes on this spreadsheet! I start every session by checking this sheet to see what everyone is up to and then I end with this sheet -- recording my work.	N/A	180	Worked with co-author (finally). Made a ton of progress but I worked a 13.5 hour day without a break if I include driving.	SD: OMG, you are a rockstar!! LS: Totally! SR: Awesome!
Thu., Feb 13, 2020	35	50	Wrote to DPR - our manscript has sat there for 17 months! This time I wrote directly to the two primary editors instead of the guy assigned to manage our paper. I got a response within seconds! But they said they will contact referees again.	SG: That is so frustrating. You're the third person (including myself) that this has happened to!		215	Working like crazy to get paper off to discussant for the Easterns	LS: Awesome! Hope to see you at the EEAs. Let's plan a coffee or lunch.	30	18	I didn't meet my goal, but I know we're sending this to a copy editor tomorrow and I have set aside the entire day to do so. Knowing I'll meet my goal makes today ok. I did procrastinate, finally sending name change forms after my marriage in July 2013!	LS: A belated congratulations on the wedding! :)
Fri., Feb 14, 2020	15	15	Hope to put in 15 minutes today. Feel like I have "writer's block." Dreading working on book rather than looking forward to it.	SD: LS, I am sure you will be great! You can do this!		65	Phew!! Finally had some time to read a paper, think and respond to co-author queries, etc. Thanks all for cheering me on!!	LS: YAY! SG: Yay! Hope my advice helped! (I sent SD my development materials, as she is overwhelmed.) SD: Thank you Sara for your materials and your tips. Super helpful!!	30	38	Wrote letter to editor about our R and R. Feeling just ok about it. They asked us to add an IV regression and I don't feel the writing is very clear in that section.	SD: The first draft is the difficult one. You can always come back to it and see if things make sense or if it needs to be clearer! I bet you are pretty much there already.

39 **Determine the amount of time and time of day/night when you need to write.** Some writers may find that they really need an hour-long (or longer) stretch of uninterrupted time in order to write productively. This may only be possible late at night or early in the morning. It is worth assessing one's particular needs and daily rhythms to decide whether such off-hours scheduling will result in more productive writing, especially if attempts to write during the standard work day have been impaired by interruptions.

40 **Divide your writing project into "hunks, chunks, and bites".** When exploring a large project, such as the actual submission of an article to a journal or the writing of a book, you don't start with the hunks, you start with the bites. But first you need to break the "hunks" into "chunks" and then "bites". Hunks are the major pieces of the project that lead to the overall goal. In the case of a journal article submission, your hunks may be something like:

- Decide which part of my research is the focus for the article
- Determine journal(s) to target
- Block the time to write
- Draft the article
- Get feedback on draft

In order to get to the manageable bite-sized level that gets your project completed, the next step is to break each hunk into a chunk. For example, drafting the article might be broken into the following chunks:

- Determine structure
- Find all pertinent notes
- Get a coach for accountability
- Mindmap the article
- Update references

The last step is to break each chunk into bites. Bites are manageable tasks and activities that can be done by one person in 5-55 minutes.

For example, "bites" from the "Update references" chunk include:

- Identify the most recent reference list.
- Move older reference lists into old, not needed folder, to avoid confusion.
- Put all physical items (articles, books) to include in the updated references onto one shelf in my office.
- Link all PDFs to include in updated references into one folder (or tag to be easily found).
- Reserve 45-minute blocks on T/Th mornings for at least the next 3 weeks.

These bites—NOT the chunks, NOT the hunks, and certainly NOT the project—are what go on your to-do list. And one bite at a time, you will actually complete your writing project.

41 **Play with words and allow your mind to be distracted—is there a memory, an image, an overheard conversation? Take time to write them down in a voice that perhaps you would not use in an academic article or pretend to be writing for your grandmother who spoke a different language.**

"Many writing advice gurus talk about writing as if it was a purely cognitive, technically imbued skill. They are wrong. I go with those who claim academic writing as an emotionally captivating, creative process and always a struggle, a problem to be solved. It's important to let the mind go free, to distract it. In doing so many new relationships and articulations begin to emerge. For a long time, I struggled with what to do with a conversation I had overheard during fieldwork. It was not enough data, I thought, to produce an article, yet I have returned often to this conversation because it was rich with evidence of how my participants perceived male-female relationships. What could I do with this evidentiary fragment? One morning for my 25-minute writing practice, I decided to write a poem and it turned out to be about my mother, a Jamaican immigrant to the U.S. She had this uncanny gift of turning leftover fabric, cheap cuts of material that she bought at a discount into beautiful stylish clothes for herself and her children. She would say, 'use what's at hand.' As I wrote this poem I began to see the connections between my mother's gift of transforming scraps into well-designed clothing and my own gut feeling that I had important ideas to contribute through my analysis of the overhead conversation. That insight shifted my thinking in such a powerful way. I began to see a way forward in writing an article using conversational analysis as the frame—the thesis sentence began to form. My mother sent her wisdom from somewhere in the universe—always looking out for her 'big daughter'."

— Gertrude J. Fraser, Associate Professor of Anthropology, University of Virginia, author of *African American Midwifery in the South: Dialogues of Birth, Race, and Memory* and several articles about diversity and inclusion in academia

42 **Handwrite a to-do list and cross out completed items.** This may seem simple in today's technological world, but there's something to be said about a hard copy to-do list and the simple act of crossing out items as you complete them. Writing out what you need to do helps organize your thoughts and ensures you aren't forgetting important items. Crossing them out gives you the satisfaction of completing them and a visual reminder of what you still need to complete.

43 **Stop procrastinating by setting micro goals.** Sometimes you aren't really having difficulty managing time but instead managing your time wisely or pushing yourself to actually sit down and write. One way to fight procrastination is to set micro goals each day—read 5 pages, write for 10 minutes, edit one page of copy, etc. If you only complete the micro goal, fine, but you will more often find that once you get started you keep going and accomplish much more than your micro goal.

44 **Find yourself an "effort buddy" who can send you a virtual trophy or thumbs up every time you get in your daily writing time.** Writing is a lonely business and there is little to show for your efforts at the end of the day. But here is a case where effort really does deserve a ribbon and a trophy! You don't have to share anything other than your effort with them and they will support you for putting in the time. Because the most productive writers are the ones who put in the effort—each and every day.

45 **Allow yourself to prioritize your research and writing over helping others.** Block out regular periods of writing time and protect them as you would other meetings and commitments. Your writing is important but can only happen if you actively allocate time to make it happen.

46 **Commit to writing for 25 minutes without distractions at least once per day (commonly referred to as the Pomodoro Technique).** You'll soon be surprised how the word count adds up. You don't need fancy apps or technology, a kitchen timer or your mobile phone is all you need. I've used the Pomodoro Technique successfully to break the cycle of distraction and procrastination that comes with a busy and varied academic workload. For me the key is giving myself permission to concentrate on just one thing for a minimum of 25 minutes. That's usually long enough to spark my interest and a productive writing session started in this way can last for two hours or more.

47 **Use a project status board as a tool for monitoring the status of projects.** Status boards can help you see all your projects in one place so that you can prioritize and plan your time. And for those who enjoy seeing their progress on a project, it can be incredibly satisfying to check off the next step in completing a major project. A project status board system can be customized to fit your needs. You can use a dry erase

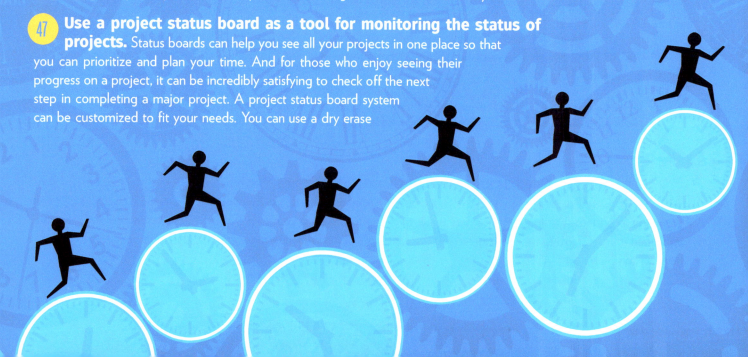

board, a self-adhesive easel pad, or a magnetic board. To set up your status board, create columns labeled Project, Status, and Comments, and list each project or component of a project underneath. List the status next to each project and use the comment column to show the next step that is needed. For example, if a book has 10 chapters and you are working on the first draft of each, you could write out the numbers 1 through 10 on the status column and circle each chapter number as the first draft is completed. Using a magnetic board allows for the addition of color-coded magnets to designate various statuses, such as first draft, final draft, out for review, etc. In situations where there is more than one author, color-coded magnets can designate who is responsible for each portion of the project. If a project is a work-for-hire and an invoice must be created, a green magnet might indicate that the invoice has been submitted.

48 **Get your goals down on paper and prioritize them.** List the various writing projects, presentations, service commitments, conferences, and books you're reading, as well as work-related projects and commitments that you anticipate working on in the coming months. You can also assign dates to the various pieces of each project you plan to accomplish. Just making a list and getting it down on paper is crucial.

Once you have completed your plan, list these projects on a whiteboard in your office, along with due dates, as appropriate. Leave plenty of space between each significant item so as to have room to make a list of the component parts. For example, if you are working on the last stages of an article, list the pieces that need to be finished: results, conclusion, references, appendices, final read-through, and submission. The best part of using a whiteboard to keep track of projects is crossing out each element as it is completed.

49 **Overcome negative thinking.** There is the voice that suggests that my "real work" (whatever that is) needs to get done first, the critical voice that tells me that I am not a very good writer anyway, and on a really bad day, the hypercritical voice that claims that I am fraud and I have no business being in a tenure-track position (imposter syndrome once again rears its ugly head). It is absolutely my responsibility to ignore all that and get busy on the particular writing task that is in front of me.

50 **Develop a writing project management chart to track all writing projects that need attention.** Part of not having enough time to write is spending too much time getting reoriented to each writing project. Most professors are working on more than one writing project at one time.

51 **Find opportunities throughout the day to do *something*.** Procrastination makes you feel overwhelmed and fearful of your writing. Small tasks help maintain momentum and just 30 minutes a day of consistent writing can produce more results than two 4-hour "binge" sessions a month. Make a list of "front burner" activities—things that take 15-30 minutes to complete—and keep the list on hand for those moments of opportunity that arise throughout the day.

52 **Create a variety of goals, both in time (daily, weekly, and monthly) and importance (deadlines, passion-based, external pressure, time needed, and long-term importance).** Be sure to make time for all of them, especially the long-term goals that are often neglected.

53 **Develop a full pipeline of projects that allow you to keep a couple of different ideas going at the same time.**

"While some may find this distracting, this gives me a place to put ideas that seem productive. Most of my projects dovetail and move my research agenda and teaching forward. If I read something that inspires a thought in one project that I plan to work on in the future, having that project in the pipeline allows me to capture that idea now instead of revisiting whatever I have read in the future and trying to regain the insights.

The project pipeline allows me to use my time differently depending on time available. For larger blocks of time, I can focus on planning and outlining. For shorter blocks of time, I can focus on writing a single paragraph or revising."

— **William Suhs Cleveland, Professor of Nonprofit Management**

54 **Determine what is important and get it done first.** Don't put off your important tasks until you have "enough time"—you likely won't.

55 **Create systems of accountability.** It's easy to break promises to yourself or to let yourself down when working toward your goals. And writing can be lonely. By creating a system of accountability and connecting with a writing partner, it's harder to let them down, even when it's your goal they're expecting you to accomplish.

56 **Pay yourself first.** Others will continue to make demands on your time, so protect your writing time as the first thing you do in the day before prepping, teaching your classes, responding to crises, or attending meetings. Even fifteen minutes at the beginning of a busy day may be enough to keep you connected to your writing project.

57 **Color Me Productive.** Scheduling is a necessary component of all writing and productivity success. When we make sure that we block off time in our schedule each day to write, we are more likely to complete our writing for the day and increase the importance we place on our writing (Goodson, 2017). How we schedule, the physical component (e.g., paper planner, online calendar, etc.) is up to personal preference, but the act of scheduling leads to success and feelings of accomplishment. While scheduling daily writing time is essential, we can increase our productivity by the way we compose our schedule. Instead of merely blocking time on the calendar each day for writing and other tasks that need completing, consider assigning a color to each type of task. For example, make writing tasks green, family responsibilities pink, teaching tasks blue, etc. Color-coding your calendar is one more step in helping you to track where your time is going. Additionally, a color-coding system can assist you in chunking your time, keeping similar tasks together when possible, and opening up larger blocks of time when available. Both of which increase time management and productivity.

58 **Celebrate your progress at every step.** Noticing what you have accomplished adds motivation. Think of your progress in the positive—what you have done—instead of beating yourself up for not accomplishing as much from your To Do list as you wanted to.

59 **Be present in case the muse decides to show up during your writing time.** This tip presumes that you schedule regular writing times, daily if possible. Schedule in writing time as you would a class or appointment.

60 **Schedule time for intrusions.** Remember the adage, "Lack of planning on your part does not constitute an emergency on my part"? When you schedule time during the day to handle emergencies, then when someone comes into your writing space or office wanting your attention right now, you can say something like, "I'll be available to help you with this at 3 p.m. [or whenever your scheduled emergency time is]".

61 **Learn to say no, without guilt if possible.** Things to say:

- "No."
- "I'm on a deadline."
- "I will consider taking that on when I have finished my book, article, etc."
- "This won't work for me." Especially when you get stuck with the majority of the work on a project for which you thought the responsibility/work would be shared.

62 **Delegate—if you are used to handling emergencies, taking the lead on a paper, etc., realize that others can grow into this position with your support.** Say "no" and delegate. Saying no without guilt takes practice. You may have to put up with uncomfortable feelings for a while, until you are used to saying no.

63 **Be clear about your priorities.** You probably don't have time to do everything really well. If publishing is a priority because you want to get your book or paper out, then avoid distractions that derail you.

64 **Can't write now? Test your assumption.** For example, if you feel too tired to write, set a timer for ten minutes and see how it goes. If you really can't write, accept it, don't feel guilty, but instead go and do something

else. If you can write, great, carry on. Common assumptions include the feeling you need to read more or do more research before you can start writing, or that there are certain times of the day (week, or year) that are best for writing. Don't assume–test it–you might surprise yourself.

65 **Prioritize writing in your life using the "rocks and pebbles" method.** If your writing always takes a back seat to more urgent or important tasks in your life you need to understand how important writing is to you so you can allocate more time to it. In short, you need to prioritize. Stephen R. Covey has a great tip. Picture an empty jar. Imagine that your life is that jar and you get to decide how to fill it. You can fill it with lots of small unimportant things, but you won't have time for what really matters. Your life is like that empty jar. You can fill it with rocks (the big important stuff), pebbles (not so important stuff) and sand (hello social media!). To make everything fit you need to put the rocks in first.

66 **Find time to write using the "traffic light" approach.** The traffic light method of scheduling helps you find the times in your week when you can, can't and might be able to do some writing. This is important because knowing when you can't write is just as important as knowing when you can. So, looking at your schedule:

1. Find your red times. Look over the next few days. Highlight all the times that you definitely can't write–when you're working, in meetings or with family. These are your no-go red times. You won't be able to write in these times so stop trying.

2. Find your amber slots. These are times in your day that might not be ideal, but you can do something. You might have distractions or be on your commute, but you can still do some useful work like researching, editing or organizing.

3. Highlight your go-go green times. These are blocks of time you can definitely write in and won't be disturbed. You probably won't have many, they probably won't be very long–but don't worry. It's your job to find them, book them in, and protect them at all costs!

Productivity

87   **Have a specific, but flexible, project plan.** Having a very specific plan is a great way to flush out what you think you would like to cover in a writing project. Creating a book proposal and chapter summaries/topics is a very helpful exercise to get you going, but it does not mean that these plans and proposals should not be flexible. Once you start writing and your style evolves, you almost certainly make many adjustments and changes to the content and order of topics covered. What you learn along the way about your topics may necessitate a shift in perspective from the time when you first crafted the proposal. In fact, a sea change is what you are likely to encounter as you dive deeper into your topic and research, but that is ok, great in fact. That is how a thesis and argument should evolve, based on the injection of new knowledge and insight.

88   **Plan ahead, splitting your workload into manageable wholes.** Vary the tasks and remember to match them with the times when you are the most productive: for some people it is the morning, for others afternoon or even evening.

89   **Tackle daily overwhelm using "decision decoupling" and "emotional decoupling".** Decision decoupling is separating the decision to do something from the action to accomplish that task. It is really the basis of morning routines. Make a habit out of a set or a series of tasks in a row, so you don't have to decide whether to do them or in what order: make the bed, brush teeth, and take a shower, for example.

With non-routine tasks, you follow the same principle: "tomorrow I'll spend an hour editing my article". That's it. Decision made. You won't then wonder if you should write another article because you already decided to edit instead of write something new. By decoupling the decision to do something

from the action of doing it, you have time to recover from the fatigue associated with making the decision before taking action. Keep it simple.

Emotional decoupling is separating the period of emotional response from the completion of related tasks. It is just as important as decision decoupling. Let's say you received difficult editing feedback. It not only involves a lot of work, but it also involves a lot of emotional labor because the critiques hurt. A normal human reaction would be to shove this away in a hidden folder on your desktop and pretend it doesn't exist. But the longer you let it sit, the longer it festers in your subconscious.

Once you've decided you'll revise the article based on the critiques, don't decide the night before you'll spend 30 minutes working on it the next morning. Yes, you've decoupled the decision to work on it from working on it, but you've underestimated the resistance you'll feel as you stare at the words like "insipid prose", or "unclear argument". Applying emotional decoupling, you will need to plan additional time to take action after initially allowing time for your emotional response to the critiques.

Here's what you could do:

SUNDAY NIGHT: Decide on a weekly plan for revision

MONDAY: Read critiques and sort into actionable tasks

TUESDAY: Address critique task 1. Do not move on to task 2.

WEDNESDAY: Address critique task 2. Do not move on to task 3.

THURSDAY: Address critique task 3. Do not move on to response memo.

FRIDAY: Write a response memo outlining your revisions.

This may seem simple, but what you've done is decouple the emotions from each critique (task). The fear of the task in its enormity is the challenge, not the actual task itself. Decoupling allows you to be kind and gentle with yourself, while still moving forward.

70 **Have a strategy, or a few strategies, rather than a specific space that signals you to write.** You won't always be able to be sure you are in the same physical spot when it is time for you to write. If some of your cues to write are portable, they will help you to write anywhere.

71 **Use a dedicated screen to show only 2 things: a timeline of project progress and writing time tracking.** By having this screen ON all the time, you can see your progress ALL the time.

72 **Find a quiet, comfortable place to work.** This way you can avoid everyday problems, at least for a few hours.

73 Create an organizational system.

"I have a bookshelf divided into cubicles, each four inches high and fourteen inches wide. I dedicate each cubicle to a chapter. In between editions, I file materials there that I find are relevant to the chapter and good candidates for inclusion in the book."

— **Karen Morris, Distinguished Professor of Law, author of twelve textbooks, a magazine column, trade books, and a publisher's blog**

74 Use the "Brainstorm Writing" technique.

But when you use this technique, don't do it alone. Find a colleague to be a "writing friend". A good writing partner is someone who is:

- An excellent writer and editor;
- A person motivated to complete project deadlines;
- A collaborator who will give you useful feedback; and
- Someone who will be able to take feedback from you.

Here's how it works:

- Once you choose your writing partner, establish mutually agreeable deadlines. The time commitment between both of you will move the project along quickly.
- Draft an outline for your writing project and assign the writing of the sections of the paper to each other.
- When your research and writing is complete, set up a day and time for collaborative editing and writing for your "brainstorm writing" session. You can either do this in person face-to-face, or you can schedule it virtually. But you must use a dual editing tool such as Google Docs during the meeting. When you meet, the writers will be sharing their ideas, phrasing and word choices. Using this technique, both authors are also able to edit simultaneously during this evaluation and critiquing process.

By using a "brainstorm writing" process, the team is able to write collaboratively and create a cohesive and well-written document. The key to being successful with this process is that both people must be comfortable accepting feedback about the writing project from each other. Having a writing partner who cannot take criticism doesn't work with this technique, because sharing feedback (both positive and negative) is critical to successful team writing. You want to make sure that after the project is completed, you will still be friends, and you have a writing partner for the future!

75 **Use the Door Hanger Barrier.** Create a simple, temporary sign as a door hanger on your office door handle and commit to hanging it on your closed office door for 90 minutes per day to keep distractions at bay. Don't say, "do not disturb writing time" as less productive colleagues somehow think it is acceptable to interrupt you. Instead, say, "In video-teleconference, please come back later" or "On Air - Recording in Progress" or "I'll be available in 90 minutes; please come back" or even, "Knock super loud, headphones in use". All of these cause casual disruptors to think twice about bothering you, especially if your office door is normally open.

76 **Identify as a writer and a creative person.** Many academics view writing as something they do rather than as part of who they are. While not all writing tasks require creativity, thinking, free writing, mind mapping or outlining, and producing drafts do. Some editing is routine but choosing the right word to convey your point is a creative endeavor.

Featured Strategy

77 **Right after finishing updates and revisions on a new edition of my textbook, I start an electronic file that includes the detailed table of contents from that recently published edition.**

"When I receive email alerts about a newly published issue from various journals in my field of industrial and organizational psychology, I look through the table of contents to see if any articles fit with an existing section in my book. If so, I paste the reference and abstract (often accessed through Google Scholar or PsycINFO) into the corresponding section of my electronic file. I also scan the table of contents to identify new topics and themes that are receiving attention in my field. Reviewing the table of contents from each issue of many journals in my field ensures that I am thinking frequently about the revision process. In fact, I am almost always on the lookout for material I can use to revise and update my textbook.

I view this continuous approach positively because I feel much more prepared when it is time to begin doing the revisions (an intensive process in itself) than if I had to search for new material and do revisions at the

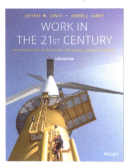

same time. Once I receive the invitation from my publisher to do the revision for the next edition, I already have a solid head start on what updates there might be for different sections of the book as well as what new themes will be included in the new edition. Although updating the textbook for each new edition is nevertheless hard work, this preparatory process helps me to get the revision up and running as quickly as possible."

— **Jeff Conte, Ph.D., author of** *Work in the 21st Century: An Introduction to Industrial and Organizational Psychology* (6e, Wiley)

78 Use the "Rule of 5's" to help you develop concepts, establish writing in the limited time you have, and produce work that is publication and presentation worthy.

- **Devote FIVE minutes or more per day to something related to your writing goals (a concept map, a literature review, drafting an outline, etc.).** Consistently visiting this idea will help it stay valid and fluid in your mind and allow you to question the work you are doing each day—something that will make you grow personally as you write.

- **Synthesize daily! Keep the synopsis of the current project to FIVE minutes or less.** If you can't explain your current writing in five minutes or less, more synthesizing, intention, and accuracy needs to take precedence. This will allow you to be more succinct in what you are trying to get across to the intended audience.

- **Read your writing for at least FIVE minutes weekly. Utilize whatever audience you may have—children, spouse, dog, neighbor, etc.** Read what you have written out loud to help you hear what you are writing and if your purpose is succinct. By reading it to others, you also get their input and will sometimes find that the questions they ask (especially from those not in your profession) drive you to explain a concept better and challenge you to address your topic more purely.

- **Simplify how you write by keeping it to FIVE main points. This works in almost any writing experience (professional or not).** Keep your outline to five main points by outlining your hand—five fingers representing the five main points of your article. The first and fifth finger represent the introduction and conclusion, but the middle three fingers or points is where the data, ideas, research, etc. can be addressed and navigated through. Tape up the paper of your hand and use it as your draft, where ideas are listed on every finger (write small). This is a visual reminder that can help you stay focused.

- **Select FIVE outcomes that your writing will produce. What or who do you want to influence, change, inform, or correct as you write?** Keeping specific outcomes invites you to write to reach a newer, higher level every single time. It should be as if those outcomes own your project, and you answer to them. Make outcomes that help you reach and grow.

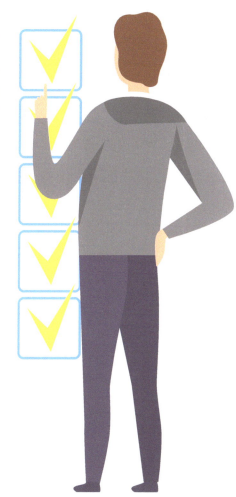

79 **Keep both a writing and productivity log to help you not only plan your writing time but also keep track of where you are in your writing and what you need to do next.** This process increases your productivity by enabling you to fill the smaller, sometimes unexpected blocks of time without any planning because you will know where you are in all of your tasks. By logging, you no longer waste time trying to remember where you left off or what you should be completing.

80 **Practice your writing regularly.** There are several methods that an author can use to induce themselves to work regularly.

- **Use self-bribery.** People can use candy or chocolate as a way to make themselves sit down to write and stay sitting down. However, that tends to pack on the pounds around the hips and tummy, so a better method is to say, "Just 15 minutes, I only have to write for 15 minutes". Once a person sits down to write, that minimal time usually expands to a longer period of time because writers tend to get into the flow of writing. The 15-minute time span for writing also helps an author to grab and make use of odd periods of time in the day when there is a break from the usual flow of activities.

- **Tell the internal critic to shut up and go away.** Arguing with the internal critic while you are trying to get words on the page is a waste of time and emotional energy. It is impossible to hurt the feelings of the internal critic and it will always come back; therefore, an author can invite the internal critic to come back when its critical abilities are needed for editing.

- **Create artificial deadlines.** Most writing projects have a real deadline. Artificial deadlines that an author sets that are in advance of the real deadline can be used to help the author preserve time before the real deadline to a) seek feedback from others before submission, and b) conduct a careful review of the written product to ensure that it meets the requirements of the writing style, journal, or publisher. In other words, it helps to avoid the practice of writing to deadline and then not having the time left to make sure the manuscript is ready for submission.

81 **Harness the power of habits for writing productivity.** Consider all three parts of the habit loop in concert—microhabit, trigger, reward.

- **Manage the microhabit.** Rather than directly starting with the end goal, begin with its kernel, or microhabit. The rules of microhabits are simple: They must be specific, easy, and completed in 1 minute or less. Consider a common writing habit goal of: I will journal daily. This is actually not very specific, nor easy, nor completed in one minute. Comparatively, I will write one paragraph in my journal before breakfast, is better. However, even more attainable is: Daily at the breakfast table, I will write one sentence.

  While obviously a one-sentence-writing-habit is not the final destination, an established microhabit can be extended, incrementally, into the actual goal. Over time (perhaps adding one sentence weekly?) you can transform such a habit, almost imperceptibly, into sustainable daily journaling. (At this modest rate, in one month, you are writing paragraphs daily). Most importantly, the scale of microhabits allow them to start at any moment. Like now.

- **Target the Trigger**—the tiny events that happen directly before writing occurred or did not occur. Triggers set a chain of actions in motion but are often outside of conscious thought. Understanding your triggers requires conducting naturalistic research with you as the subject. Returning to the hypothetical goal of daily breakfast-time journaling, perhaps in Week 1, you ultimately wrote for 4 of 7 days. Therefore, consider the 3 days that you did not write. What happened exactly before you chose a different direction? Did you check your email? Did you decide that you would be more focused with a nap? Did the phone ring? Once you know your negative triggers, you can be proactive to prevent them. Perhaps you set a policy of internet start time; or set an evening alarm to remind yourself to go to bed; or silence your phone at breakfast.

  Equally important is to study the positive triggers on the days when you wrote exactly as planned: What action had just happened? Where were you? Who else was around? Where was your phone? Use that information to try to duplicate your success. Maybe your positive trigger was a strategically placed sticky note on the coffee pot, or a "writing alarm" on your phone. Once you can identify what triggers assist in your habit building, then you can capitalize on them. Alternatively, like any ritual, you can design one to support the behavior that you are aiming at.

- **Reward yourself for writing.** It may require some experimentation to get the right reward sorted out, because the most obvious rewards, like chocolate, may create other problems if overdone. Therefore, think beyond food. The process of tracking and watching growth over time is intrinsically rewarding. (If you've experienced the happiness of your fitness band buzzing on your wrist, you know this to be true!) For writing, logs that automatically tally your minutes or words can be highly sustaining. Social reinforcements are also highly motivating, so having an immediate check-in (virtual or real) provides accountability and a cheerful word. Alternatively, going for a short walk can cap a writing routine, with the outdoor time providing a natural mood boost. Again, the goal is that the reward will become a craving that helps to enliven the cue.

82 **Try to focus on one chapter or "assignment" at a time, completing that as much as possible.** Break down tasks into more manageable parts and make a list you can check off and feel good about. Try to identify start and stopping points so you can easily pick up where you left off.

83 **If you are having difficulty writing, be flexible.** Get up and leave it and then return to the writing after having readjusted your "stop" time.

84 **Dress for work if you write at home.** Put on "work clothes" (however you define that). Don't write in your PJs.

85 **When it comes to proofreading, make a check-off list so that you cover each and every task in the proper order for each and every page that needs to be proofread.** Do not vary from this list to minimize the chance of missing errors.

86 **Use multiple monitors when writing.** The use of multiple monitors prevents the need of "layering" documents on the monitor and (possibly) getting lost in the depth of the open folders, documents, etc. Use three monitors on your desktop computer when writing: the one in front of you can have the latest draft of the document that you are writing; the monitor to your left can have the previous draft of that document so that you can refer back to that as you are rewriting the latest draft; and the monitor to your right (which can be the smallest) can have the important files and folders open for the current project.

87 **When working at home around family members (and pets), consider including them rather than pushing them away as you write.** Writing projects involve long stretches of focused attention. Other household members—adults, children, and even pets—sometimes have trouble remembering and honoring boundaries when you need to concentrate on writing. Such distractions can be minimized by:

- **Using an inbox/outbox system where a family member can leave you a note (or crayon drawing) when they need your attention.** Commit to responding to inbox items during your regular breaks and you may find that your rate of being disturbed will drop.

- **Setting up a workspace near yours for your children to work on drawing projects or other fun activities.** These could be for their own enjoyment or could be described as projects that will help you in your work, such as, "I'm thinking of including a picture of a boat in my book/article. Can you draw me a boat to give to the illustrator?"

- **Creating a comfy space very near your workstation—such as a small pet bed between your keyboard and monitor—to provide pets with**

connection with you as you focus on writing. Using your regular breaks to scratch and/or play with an attention-seeking pet may be enough for them to avoid disturbing you while you are writing.

- **Holding a "family meeting" in which your household members hear about your writing project and are asked for suggestions on how they can contribute.** Offer that honoring a "Writing In Progress" door hanger and the inbox/outbox system is a way for them to contribute. Once everyone is agreed, post a short synopsis of that agreement where everyone can see it—perhaps on the door of your home office, kitchen bulletin board, or on the side of your portable file box.

Featured Strategies

88 **Trigger imagination and awaken all senses by going out for "Beethoven's Walks".** "I purposely go by myself to explore ideas, discard some of them, and find new ones that may be triggered by chance or by something my eyes catch while I'm in motion. This used to be one of Beethoven's practices in Vienna to allow a composition to work through his brain. I believe my writing process is much more effective/inspiring if I do it away from a screen. I can also envision the full structure of what I want to do, instead of dwelling on immediate details."

89 **Use voice memo on your phone to make lists of writing topics.** "This way you have a catalogue of options to choose from when you need to come up with content under a quick deadline. Being able to store ideas on the go is extremely helpful. Talking through, instead of writing them, allows me to flow through ideas in a conversational tone. I can explore questions or move into variations of the subject without thinking about grammar, tone, or even order. I'm just talking to myself, so ideas are presented in their purest form."

90 **Go to bed early and wake up at 3 or 4 a.m. to write.** "I don't do this often, but it seems to me that I accomplish more between 4-6 a.m. than the rest of the day if I don't wake up early. At that time, I have a fresh brain and no distractions, no family members walking around, no neighbors listening to music, no social media."

91 **Give yourself quick deadlines to meet within the hour.** "For me, that might be research timelines, writing a portion of the paper, or recording a determined number of musical bars. If I fulfill my goal, I can feel accomplished and that makes me want to keep going."

— Daniel Pardo, Assistant Professor of Flute, Prairie View A&M University, Yamaha Performing Artist & Clinician

92 **Make time for yourself.** Give yourself 10-20 minutes when you are able to be totally alone somewhere you feel relaxed and comfortable. During this period of time, you should let everything go, take a nap, or practice deep breathing or meditation to ease your mind and relax your body.

93 **Continually gather new ideas and content.** File it so that when you're ready to write, you have reference information on hand. That cuts down on research time and allows you to focus on the writing process.

94 **Write for 20 minutes (freehand or typing) as the first thing you do upon waking up.** It does not need to necessarily be on a specific passage or writing project, just any writing to get the juices flowing.

95 **Change up how you write.** In the same way some might find it useful to change physical locations when writing, try writing on your phone or another device instead of your computer. This can help tremendously especially in the middle of deadline stress.

96 **Prioritize which tasks are worthy of your resources of time, talent, energy, and attention.** Although there are tasks that we all have to do because they support what we want to do—such as filing your grades from the last semester—you should be spending most of your time doing things you choose to do and that are fun to do. Develop a Dream Book or Wall to keep all of your goals parked so that you can pick and choose which ones get your attention and other resources. Procrastinate creatively so you can make time, energy, and space for professional activities, including research and writing. Plan backward and estimate time-to-completion more accurately.

Adapted from: "Don't manage time, manage goals." TAA Blog, *Abstract* (April 2011).

97 **Determine your purpose for writing.** Many people say that one day they want to write a book. The reality is that most never follow through on that dream. People use life and its ongoing obstacles as an excuse for never starting their journey to becoming a published author. Like anything else in life, writing is a skill. It takes research and practice to get to a point where you can put words onto paper. Before you even begin you should first decide why you want to write a book since writing comes from inside you. If you are not motivated and do not prepare or possess the knowledge and skills required to write a book you will likely fail. Writing is a lonely and time-consuming process. If you get into it for the wrong reason you face "writers block", stress, frustration, and ultimately may give up on your dream.

People write for many reasons and you must decide yours. Some common reasons include:

- Fame and fortune
- Self-esteem
- Share personal experiences with others
- Help others
- Leave a legacy for family and friends

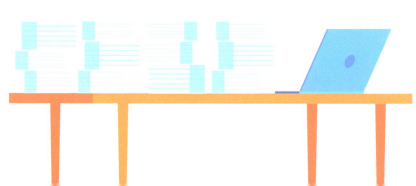

98 **Become knowledgeable about the textbook authoring and publishing process.** As a textbook author your content must be informative, accurate, and presented in a logical fashion. It must also conform to pedagogical standards and formats used in academic and textbook publications. Additionally, your message must be delivered in a manner that holds the attention of your readers.

It is not enough to be an expert in your field or good instructor. Those are different skill sets. Before writing a book, successful authors research information about the profession, attend courses and conferences for writers, and learn about the writing and publishing process. Some helpful topics relate to writing, editing, contract negotiation, book marketing, sales, and personal branding.

99 **Resist the greatest enemy of writing in higher education: Email.** Ask yourself, will writing email get you published or promoted? Do you want your academic epitaph to read, "Lived a Happy Life Checking & Writing Email"? Kidding aside, don't start your day with Email. Instead, spend the first 40 minutes of your day working only on one research-related writing action item. Don't know which writing-related action item to work on for 40 minutes? Please answer this question: what is one writing-related activity I can do in 40 minutes before I check email? Finally, express thanks for starting the day with your thoughts and writing.

100 **Make sure that no matter how hard it is, you've made a step towards your "true to yourself" goals every day.** The goal is not to control time to achieve, but to control your focus to achieve. Let every day be your New Year's resolution day.

101 **Write.** Make a list of chapter titles and topic titles and then go to it, ticking them off your list as you go. Revise and edit your work time and time again. The more you edit it the better it gets. But first, all you need to do is write.

102 **Be inspired by current events.** From the news to what's on various apps, to the newspaper and other reading content, you can be motivated to write when you view what is going on around you. Some authors, for example, do journaling which is a good daily or weekly habit. Just write about something going on in your community or some development in your field or discipline this year, for example.

103 **Break down your projects into bite-size pieces.**

"I plan most of my projects 6 months in advance using a Gantt Chart. First, I create the project I need to complete, such as a writing project. Next, I break it down into tasks on the vertical axis. I list every task I need to complete to finish the project. Next, on the horizontal axis, I list the time required to complete each task. If I am writing a research article or a book chapter, I plot out a certain time, week, or month. I indicate a start and end date and connect them using a horizontal line.

Below the Gantt Chart, I list important dates and milestones. On my monthly calendar, I focus on a task that needs to be accomplished for that project (i.e., research or an interview for an upcoming article or book). I divide monthly tasks into weekly tasks. So, each week I dedicate 30 to 60 minutes to that task (e.g., research, compiling, and writing). I keep separate files for each task. My Gantt Chart helps me accomplish several tasks in a six-month period to complete any goal or project I set for myself."

— **Dr. Derrick C. Darden, Professor of Human Management, Tiffin University**

104 **Keep learning.** Sometimes you feel inspired to learn deeply about a topic or discipline and that makes you want to write further. From a few thoughts, you end up with a few pages and enjoy exploring the discipline. Taking online courses, reading books and also seeing finished works, may make you delve into writing something original and thought-provoking.

105 **Enlist the help of a writing buddy at home or at your place of work.** You can remind each other of your writing goals or coach each other. You can also motivate each other when you feel despondent or unsatisfied with your written outcomes. Your writing buddy can also do things like edit your work, provide feedback and offer writing advice too.

106 Take advantage of "thinking time". Because writing is a creative act that involves (among other things) making novel connections, referencing other authors, carefully choosing words, and developing a persuasive argument, a writer can't assume critical eureka moments will occur within a rigidly set time frame. The act of thinking does not abide by arbitrary schedules and time sheets. To get more out of those precious segments of the day set aside for writing, a writer may need to bring with them fragments of thought that occurred at some other unplanned time. Equipped with the ideas that came while taking a shower, waiting for a train, or having a cup of coffee, for example, can empower an author when they finally sit down behind a computer to officially write.

107 Capture ideas while on the go using your iPhone Notes app. Using something as simple as the "Notes" app on an iPhone can be incredibly valuable. Whole sections to chapters can be written on the fly and freely available when the previously scheduled time to write is about to begin. Think of it as a way to "hit the ground running". A writer should be ready to capture those invaluable moments of inspiration whenever and wherever they occur. Doing so will make carefully managed time for writing much more productive.

108 Have an accountability partner that you share your progress with. Just going through that process can help keep you on track and make sure you don't disappoint yourself or your accountability partner.

109 Turn off notifications on your computer and phone. Turn everything off—social media, text, emails, voicemails—so that you can write. That is your writing and research time. This distraction control keeps chaos at bay and gives you permission to be focused on your work.

110 Take breaks. Getting up, going for a walk around the block, getting a fresh cup of tea from the kitchen, all of those breaks will help you stay productive and give you new perspective on your writing. Standing desks and walking desks are excellent alternatives to endless sitting. Keep in mind your eyes also periodically need breaks. Look away from your computer screen and focus on something else within your office.

111 Do not ignore ergonomics. Improper ergonomics—how you are positioned at your workstation—can put enormous stress on your body.

112 Use writing accelerators. To keep your writing flowing, use hints like "cite here" or bullet points that show where you are headed next before you finish your writing session for the day. To mark your place for where you should start the next day, place three asterisks. Use the find feature of your word processing software (CTRL-F) to locate the asterisks. This will save you the time of having to scroll to where you left off and from getting distracted by the urge to edit.

113 Keep a virtual filing cabinet. Services like Dropbox and Google Drive allow you to access your documents from any web-enabled device anywhere, anytime. This allows you to work on any given project no matter where you are. Just as you would organize a physical filing cabinet in your home with various folders, so too should you create virtual folders for research, writing, and your CV.

114 Save online material as a PDF. Saving information in the form of a PDF is much cleaner and easier to navigate than saving it as HTML. Some programs that allow you to save files as PDFs: Adobe Acrobat, PDFLite, and Google Docs.

115 **Utilize a reference control system.** Various bibliographic online management tools, such as Mendeley, EndNote, and Zotero, can help you store and organize your references. You can even keep a master Microsoft Word or Excel file for references you use most frequently.

116 **Create multiple drafts starting with a zero draft.**

- *Zero draft:* This is where you make a list of ideas, make a mind map, or freewrite whatever comes to mind for you on the topic.

- *Zero+ draft:* In this step, you put some hierarchy to the ideas from your zero draft. Here you put your note cards or assorted sticky notes in order with main idea categories and sub-ideas under the main ideas.

- *1st draft:* This is the step where you put your ideas into paragraph form, adding even more hierarchy of ideas and concepts. Perhaps an outline fits here before you write paragraphs. You start each paragraph with a topic sentence (general) and add additional, more specific sentences to each paragraph.

- *2nd draft:* Now you are ready to start adding headings to your paper, introductory and summary paragraphs to each section, and topic sentences to your paragraphs. Write transitions from one section to another when you need them. Review the whole paper for internal logic; for instance, if you stated a purpose for your research or paper in the Introduction, pay attention to how you followed through with that in later chapters of the paper. Finish formatting. Spell check. These things make your organization clear to the reader and make your paper easy to follow.

- *3rd draft:* Finally, you proofread your paper, catching the mistakes that spell check didn't catch, changing wording to get closer to what you meant to say. Maybe you give a copy of your paper to a friend to read so that you can get feedback for corrections. After this final proofreading and editing, your paper is ready to submit.

- *Additional drafts:* You may look at the third draft and change the language to add terminology that is particular to the field of study or to the type of writing you are doing once you have the ideas down. Or you send your really good third draft to an agent or publishing house editor, who wants a slightly different style or somewhat different content. This alternative may result in your dropping back to a first or second draft situation. If you do use these additional draft options, make sure you have rechecked on the items listed above for 2nd and 3rd drafts before you send off your paper.

117 **Be willing to quit when, or even before, you reach diminishing returns.** Many people find that getting exhausted from writing does not motivate them to do more writing. Notice how long you can write before you get too tired or too self-critical or writing is just plain no longer fun.

118 **Find a good metaphor to use to get you into your writing space.** One person whose writing space was upstairs imagined that she was climbing a mountain to her private writing space. Another visualized his writing space as a fertile field, just waiting for him to plant it with words and ideas. Others named their projects, as in "I'm going to spend some time with Sally now".

119 **Acknowledge author loneliness and find a way to mitigate it.** If you crave more social time, you might join or start a "Shut up and write" (SUAW) gathering. Usually these last for a predetermined amount of time. Group members spend a few (like 5) minutes telling the others what their goals for the writing session are. Then people silently write for the predetermined amount of time. After the SUAW time is up, group members may leave or socialize. A modification of SUAW is to have a writing buddy to check in with initially and to share your progress with at the end of the predetermined writing session. You can do SUAW and writing buddies in a shared space or online.

120 **Make self-care a priority.** Expecting yourself to do good work when you are tired, hungry, ill, burned out, or craving social contact may be unrealistic. Self-care is an investment in yourself and in your writing project.

121 **Edit last.** Get down the information with citation notes and go back and tighten up your writing and citation later. What you need to aim for initially is paragraphs of content rather than perfect sentences.

122 **Enlist the support of others with a visual reminder.** TAA supplies members with a doorknob hanger that reads, "Please do not disturb. Writing in progress." Some people put a slider sign on the door to their writing space. Others tell their colleagues, students, family, "If I'm wearing my ball cap, don't talk to me, even if you see me in the restroom."

123 **Make a list of short activities you can do when you feel too tired/busy/burned out to be creative.** Instead of telling yourself that you don't have time to get into your writing project today, you can tell yourself that you'll spend 15 minutes checking footnotes.

124 **Find an accountability partner.** Accountability to someone other than yourself can really help. Join a writing group or hire a writing coach. Tell your group or your coach what you plan to accomplish in the coming week.

125 **Keep a writing journal to note your progress, where to start the next time you sit down to write, and as a place to note down things that could have interrupted you that you will tend to later.** By keeping a writing journal, you can begin immediately by writing, not thinking—it's low hanging fruit—each time you sit down to write. A writing journal will help you learn how much you write in a sitting. It is a measurable way to keep track of what you are actually getting done. It also helps break a big project down into smaller more manageable pieces.

126 **Look at your collaboration efforts with co-authors and / or co-editors as a series of activities for which each person might volunteer or be assigned.** For example, project manager (likely the first author/editor), first (second, and third) writer for particular sections, meeting facilitator and agenda keeper, content editor/s, style editor/s, correspondent with publisher, time/date keeper to facilitate remaining on deadline, and the like. When people have clearly outlined tasks, the collaborative project is more apt to be developed with clarity and on time. A critical part of this work is to make sure that communication remains open whether through email, texting, phoning, video conferencing, or all of the above. If three or more people are involved, even when only two need to talk, the others need to be advised that a discussion happened, why it was needed, and what was decided if a decision was made. It is also crucial to determine what it means to be first or second author/editor. If there are two people, will they be handling the same amount of work (50/50) or will one, because of being "first" named, take on more of the work (60/40 or 55/45)? If there are three or more involved authors/editors, what will be their ranking, why will it be that way, and how will they carry out their work together? If the collaboration fails for any reason, ultimately, the first author/editor

might need to take more responsibility to get the project done satisfactorily and posted to the publisher on time. Finally, successful collaboration relies on trust, which must be developed from the outset. Trust is facilitated by regular meetings—perhaps scheduled for the same time weekly for the project's duration—that are opened with respectful interpersonal chat to remind co-authors and co-editors of why they elected to work together and why they care to complete the project together.

127 **Use cloud-based software like Google Docs, which allows multiple authors to work simultaneously on collaborative projects.** It helps both with the actual document creation as well as with managing the overall project because people can look online together—synchronously—and adjust time/dates and other work. That said, such collaboration still can occur through asynchronous document sharing using tracked changes and comments and posting it via email. "Old fashioned", so to speak, still works.

128 **Develop a writing streak.** The streak, well known in running circles, is a great way to encourage you to show up every day, put in the requisite mile(s), and feel like something significant, even if small, was accomplished. One common running challenge put forth by a major running publication involves running at least one mile every day between Memorial Day and Independence Day. While the goal is to simply run one mile a day, oftentimes the runner, while they're at it, will run more. At the end of each day, the runner has accomplished something while remaining focused on a bigger goal (completion of the streak). And of course, accomplishing the bigger goal should come with a larger reward...signing up for a destination race, as an example.

One of the biggest challenges writers face is the activation energy of getting started. Life gets hectic, other work piles up, meetings abound, and the writer may not feel like they have much to say right now anyway. And yet, deadlines loom. The idea of a writing streak helps to overcome these many barriers to productivity. By setting a goal (2,000 words per day, edit 15 pages per day, draw 15 figures per day, work on the project for 1 hour per day), the writer is forced to sit down at the desk and do something/anything. The larger goal demands that even if it's 10 p.m. and the writer is exhausted, the streak must be kept alive. Many times, the writer starts off these sessions just going through the motions, hoping to check whatever artificial box has been created. Fifteen minutes in, the writer has found a rhythm and real, meaningful, and productive work is being done. Before you know it, the goal of words/pages/hours worked is surpassed and the streak continues.

Over time, the writing streak breaks down all activation barriers by changing the goal. The goal is no longer to "write the perfect chapter" but is instead, to "keep the streak alive" so that the larger reward is achieved. And no, the larger reward of the writing streak isn't the completion of a project or even a perfect chapter. There will be many streaks that accumulate to make these bigger achievements possible. The reward of each streak is the special dinner, the weekend getaway, or perhaps a trip to the next TAA conference where you can share your successes and challenges with other authors...a double victory!

Time Management & Productivity Templates

Bi-Weekly Writing Tool. "This is a two-week graphic organizer that keeps track of which projects I've worked on, and in which weeks. I prioritize the top three items for the week and list them in the far-left column, and then list everything else below it. I place a checkmark in the box for each day that I spent 50 minutes or more on that project. My goal is to touch three different projects each day."

— **Dr. Kathy B. Ewoldt, Assistant Professor of Special Education, University of Texas at San Antonio**

Bi-Weekly Writing Tracking Tool

Contributed by Kathy Ewoldt, Kathy.ewoldt@utsa.edu

Dates: _____

This Week's Goals: _____

Project	M	T	W	Th	F	S/S
1)						
2)						
3)						
Everything else						

Daily Goal: Touch 3 different projects, 30 min each.

Dates: _____

This Week's Goals: _____

Project	M	T	W	Th	F	S/S
1)						
2)						
3)						
Everything else						

Daily Goal: Touch 3 different projects, 30 min each.

Monthly Goal Setting Worksheet. "Every month, my colleagues and I use this worksheet to post our goals and check each other's progress at the end of the month."

— Burcu Izci, Assistant Professor, Early Childhood Education

Monthly Goal Setting Worksheet

Month:

Goals	Progress	Task Accomplished or Not?
Writing / Research Projects		
Teaching		
Committee Work		
Personal Goals		

Contributed by Burcu Izci, Assistant Professor, Early Childhood Education

Academic Writing Checklist. "I complete this checklist as one of my final steps before submitting a paper for review. This checklist assists me in remembering little details that can sometimes get overlooked."

— Wendi K. Zimmer, Professor of Writing and Communication

Academic Writing Checklist

_____ ① **Paragraph Structure:** Does each paragraph have only one key sentence and all other sentences support that one key sentence?

_____ ② **Transitions:** Do you have transition words/sentences between and within each paragraph so your reader can follow your writing?

_____ ③ **Antecedent:** Check for usage of the words this, that, these, and those making sure you need them and they are referenced. For example: This is great! (What is great?)

_____ ④ **Voice:** Do a word find for passive verbs (is, was, will be, and were). Try to change these to active verbs.

_____ ⑤ **Wordiness:** Search for the word "of" and shorten or eliminate "of" phrases, as well as other unnecessary words, to make your text move faster and easier to read.

_____ ⑥ **Headers:** Do your headers clearly align to the focus of your paper and clearly connect to the idea before and after the header.

_____ ⑦ **Subject-Verb Agreement:** Are they both singular or both plural? They must match within a sentence.

_____ ⑧ **Sentence Structure:** Do your sentences start in different ways and vary in length?

_____ ⑨ **Audience:** Who is your audience? Have you kept them in mind while you wrote?

_____ ⑩ **Formatting:** Does your paper follow correct formatting requirements? (Double-spaced, 12 pt., Times New Roman font, etc.)

_____ ⑪ **Examples:** Well placed examples help your reader better understand the concept you are discussing and clarifies your thinking.

_____ ⑫ **Terminology:** Are all essential terms clearly defined or explained?

_____ ⑬ **Argument:** Do you have an argument? Strong writing presents an argument that is clear and well developed.

_____ ⑭ **Claims:** Do you support the claims you make with sources or just make claims? Are your sources cited correctly? (in-text, and Reference page)

_____ ⑮ **Consistency:** Does your introduction and conclusion deliver the same message as the remainder of your paper?

_____ ⑯ **Reverse Outline:** Copy and paste the key sentence of each paragraph, in order, in a separate document. Does the order make sense? If not, rearrange the order of your paragraphs.

_____ ⑰ **Grammar:** Use a free online resource, like grammarly.com, to check your paper for proper mechanics use.

_____ ⑱ **Read it Out Loud:** When you think you are done, read the entire paper out loud to yourself or a friend. This practice will help you catch little mistakes often missed.

Contributed by Wendi K. Zimmer, Professor of Writing and Communication

DEADLINE

Writing Group Template. "I created a shared Google Sheet with colleagues who are also working on writing projects. It has four columns for each member—Daily goal in minutes, Actual time spent writing, Own comments on your work, Others' comments on your work. Each row is a new day. Use it to comment on your own work and to give each other words of encouragement. Having colleagues review your goals and your ups and downs gives you a sense of community—you are not in this alone. Plus, it keeps you motivated."

— **Lisa Daniels, Professor of Economics and International Studies, Washington College**

Writing Group Template

Contributed by Lisa Daniels, Professor of Economics and International Studies, Washington College

Date	Participant:				Participant:				Participant:			
	Goal Minutes	Actual Minutes	Own Comments	Others' Comments	Goal Minutes	Actual Minutes	Own Comments	Others' Comments	Goal Minutes	Actual Minutes	Own Comments	Others' Comments

Weekly Time Tracking Calendar.

"During the academic year, the calendar function in my cellphone is sufficient in helping me to track my schedule. In summertime, however, to keep myself on track, I use this Weekly Time Tracking Calendar in Word. I include certain tasks/activities to do daily and assign an approximate amount of time to accomplish them. I print out this document weekly to track what I have or have not done and to adjust for the next week accordingly. This helps me keep up with and evaluate my progress."

— Chin-Nu Lin, Professor of Nursing, author of several nursing scholarly articles

Weekly Time Tracking Calendar

Week of:

MONDAY

TASK/ACTIVITY	TIME
1)	
2)	
3)	
4)	
5)	
6)	
7)	
8)	
9)	
10)	

TUESDAY

TASK/ACTIVITY	TIME
1)	
2)	
3)	
4)	
5)	
6)	
7)	
8)	
9)	
10)	

WEDNESDAY

TASK/ACTIVITY	TIME
1)	
2)	
3)	
4)	
5)	
6)	
7)	
8)	
9)	
10)	

THURSDAY

TASK/ACTIVITY	TIME
1)	
2)	
3)	
4)	
5)	
6)	
7)	
8)	
9)	
10)	

FRIDAY

TASK/ACTIVITY	TIME
1)	
2)	
3)	
4)	
5)	
6)	
7)	
8)	
9)	
10)	

SAT / SUN

TASK/ACTIVITY	TIME
1)	
2)	
3)	
4)	
5)	
6)	
7)	
8)	
9)	
10)	

Contributed by Chin-Nu Lin, Professor of Nursing, author of several nursing scholarly articles

Scholarship Tracking Chart.

"This tracking chart lists projects by idea or title in the left-hand column. The second column from the left is where the possible publication outlet is listed— either the journal title or an academic press. The column noting 'Possible Scholars Who Might Read This' is for listing those in discipline or subfield who are interested in this topic or have already done scholarship on the topic. The Notes section is for putting in links to publication information, tasks that should be done on this project, and next steps (for example, emailing a co-author for clarification). The Status column is for noting the stage of the project."

— Christine Tulley, Professor of English, author of *How Writing Faculty Write*, and Coach, Defend & Publish, LLC

Collaborative Writing Log.

"This writing log is relatively self-explanatory and easily adapted and revised to meet other collaborative group needs. It enables writers to report on their activities at the end of their workdays, and it encourages both useful self-reflection and staying on top of the writing process given that everyone is able to view the project's overarching process."

— Beth L. Hewett, PhD. President and Executive Coach, Defend & Publish, LLC, academic coaches for adult writers. Author of numerous books and articles

Scholarship Projects Tracking Chart (Referenced in "It's July, Have You Started Writing Yet?" in *Inside Higher Education*)

Tag #	Accepted and finished, but not published yet	Tag #	Calls for papers with approaching deadlines	Tag #	Active projects
	Tag #	Ideas and projects without set timeline	Tag #	Submitted and waiting to hear back	

TAG	PROJECT / NEW IDEA	Possible Publication/ Presentation Outlet(s)	Scholars Who Might Read This	Deadline	NOTES	STATUS (idea, drafted, sent in, in R&R, etc.)

Contributed by Christine Tulley, Professor of English, author of How Writing Faculty Write, and Coach, Defend & Publish, LLC.

Collaborative Writing Log

Contributed by Beth L. Hewett, PhD. President and Executive Coach, Defend & Publish, LLC, academic coaches for adult writers. Author of numerous books and articles.

Author:

Date	Time on Writing	Date Section or Chapter Due to Group	Daily Subgoal (content, organization, edit)	Progress Made	Challenges/ Writer's Reflections	Co-authors' Comments & Suggestions	Next Steps

Author:

Date	Time on Writing	Date Section or Chapter Due to Group	Daily Subgoal (content, organization, edit)	Progress Made	Challenges/ Writer's Reflections	Co-authors' Comments & Suggestions	Next Steps

Backwards Planning Worksheet. "I use a modified version of Susan Robison's backwards planning template (from her book *Peak Performing Professor*) based on the concept that all work flows from the end, in this case the submission deadline, whether self- or externally-imposed.

I enter the deadline at the bottom of the page, then work backwards in time and up the page to create the along-the-way intermediate tasks that allow me to meet the final deadline. I use a weekly set-up for my backward plan, with each week being one row in a table. I have a checklist of more-time-needed-than-anticipated tasks that I use to make sure my backward plan is complete (e.g., checking the manuscript against common APA errors using Onwuegbuzie et al. 2010, formatting to the journal's preference, verifying DOIs for references, checking for strong and active verbs, copy editing a print version).

The backwards planning approach helps me get real—real fast—about that long-in-the-future deadline and prioritize my writing tasks for each week. Also, by identifying the weekly tasks in advance, I forgo the procrastination involved in deciding on next steps. If I get stuck on a particular task, or must wait for a collaborator, I move down the table to the next task. This approach allows the project to keep moving forward.

A typical backward plan for a journal article or conference paper for which the data are collected and analyzed already, or for which the project is already well-developed, might be 10 or 12 weeks long, so 10 or 12 rows on the table. For less-developed projects, or when data collection and analyses are needed, the backwards plan might be 25 or even 30 weeks long.

Because I've saved previous backwards plans, I can build a new backwards plan quickly using simple cut-and-paste actions. It's no surprise that the backward plan is useful in academic writing, because at its essence, the backwards plan is a simple project management tool applicable to all types of projects.

The genius of Dr. Robison's application of the backward plan is to conceive of academic writing as a project to be accomplished, not a regular (and challenging) task to be tolerated. I've applied the backwards plan to submitting a manuscript to a white paper series with no explicit deadline, completing my full professor portfolio, submitting countless conference papers, finishing an R&R manuscript, submitting a grant proposal, creating a national-level workshop and resources, and completing this contribution, among other tasks."

— **Ella L. Ingram, Associate Dean for Professional Development and Professor of Biology, Rose-Hulman Institute of Technology**

Backwards Planning Worksheet

This strategy is adapted from:
Robison, S. (2013). The peak performing professor:
A practical guide to productivity and happiness. Jossey-Bass.

Start at the end/submission date, determine key steps GOING BACKWARDS, insert known conflicts, account for likely slow-down from external events (e.g., advisor), identify major tasks in appropriate order GOING BACKWARDS using specific verbs, then break major tasks into absurdly small units.

Example of Backwards Planning for a Full Professor Portfolio

By the end of the week beginning...	I will have...
May 15	read three framing papers for professional development section; drafted the professional development narrative; created "standard response paragraphs" for evaluations; cross-checked CV with PTR File; drafted schedule of responses for evaluations
May 22	made progress as committed on student evaluation responses; read two framing papers for professional development section; re-drafted the professional development narrative; incorporated evidence into professional development narrative
May 29	edited and completed the professional development narrative; acquired raw and aggregated data from assessment office for student evaluations; made progress as committed on student evaluation responses
June 5	requested letters of support from XX, YY, ZZ, AA, BB, CC; made progress as committed on student evaluation responses; created four alternate figures for student evaluation scores; checked with colleague about alternate figures
June 12	field-tested figures of evaluations with accountability group; made progress as committed on student evaluation responses; drafted outline of teaching narrative; read three framing papers for teaching section
June 19	made progress as committed on student evaluation responses; drafted narrative of teaching section; read two framing papers for teaching section;
June 26	done nothing new due to conference travel
July 3	completed all responses to evaluations; created the argument about responding to evaluations; incorporated evidence into teaching narrative; reviewed three examples portfolios
July 10	edited and completed the teaching narrative; drafted the service statement; checked in with letter writers; read three framing papers about the service narrative
July 17	incorporated evidence into the service section; edited and completed the service statement
July 24	drafted an executive summary
July 31	edited and completed an executive summary; inserted letters of support; requested quick review from department head
Aug 7	assembled PDF; requested a reading by at least two trusted colleagues; cross-checked all included documents to PTR File; emailed/uploaded documents for PTR File
Aug 14	updated all internal links, bookmarks, references, etc.
Aug 21	addressed comments regarding communication approach; read the portfolio in its entirety looking for errors
Aug 28	remedied all formatting, grammatical, and other errors; submitted the portfolio; drank at least one margarita; and danced a jig

Features of the project to consider in making the backward plan

- Time away: vacation, conferences, retreats, medical leave, other obligations
- Buffer for slow-down by collaborators
- Work burden for other areas: grading, course development, committee work
- What tasks generally take you a long time
- The number of revisions you are likely to implement
- The amount of reading you need to do to be up-to-date
- The learning curve associated with new software
- Emotionally stressful aspects
- Periodic "30,000-foot reviews"

Activities that take more time than anticipated

- Formatting for print or journal specs
- Checking against common errors
- Copy editing
- Formatting to Science of Scientific Writing specs
- Verifying DOIs for all references
- Writing cover letter
- Submitting via online portal
- Writing the opening paragraph
- Writing the closing paragraph
- Compiling budget information (for grants)
- Compiling personnel information (for grants)
- Crafting the most effective title, keywords, and abstract
- Negotiating authorship with collaborators
- Meeting with collaborators
- Tracking down critical but obscure references

Contributed by Ella L. Ingram, Associate Dean for Professional Development and Professor of Biology, Rose-Hulman Institute of Technology

Backwards Planning Worksheet

Contributed by Ella L. Ingram, Associate Dean for Professional Development and Professor of Biology, Rose-Hulman Institute of Technology

Project:

By the end of the week beginning...	I will have...

DEADLINE: COMPLETION:

References

Onwuegbuzie, A. J., Combs, J. P., Slate, J. R., & Frels, R. K. (2010). Editorial: Evidence-based guidelines for avoiding the most common APA errors in journal article submissions. *Research in the Schools*, 16(2), ix-xxxvi.

Robison, S. (2013). *The peak performing professor: A practical guide to productivity and happiness*. Jossey-Bass.

Software Recommendations

Asana. "This online project management tool is free for workgroups of up to 15 people and allows the user to attach files, assign tasks, set deadlines, and manage complex projects. When used by an author (or co-authors), this tool can help track the minutiae of details necessary when writing a textbook or conducting research for an academic article. Multiple projects may be tracked, so Asana can be used for anything from writing a textbook to ordering office supplies. A mobile app is available, so projects may be managed from anywhere." [https://asana.com]

— **Mike Kennamer, community college dean and academic and textbook author**

Beeminder. "This goal-tracking software helps you set realistic to-do lists or goals and forces you to complete them or you are charged money when your goal is not accomplished." [https://www.beeminder.com]

— **Thrishika Potan, CIE graduate student at Loyola Academy, author of published nutrition-based journal article, writer and content creator**

Clockify. "I use this time tracking app to manage my working hours. When I have multiple deadlines in one day, using Clockify reminds me that my workday is not as long as I think it is. This can be very encouraging, as I sometimes have to sort through 4000+ words of content a day." [https://clockify.me]

— **Dallas Glenn, freelance academic author, writer, editor, and proofreader**

Digital Assistants (Alexa, Google, Siri). "I set a timer on my Echo Dot and write for a specific amount of time. Usually, by the time my timer goes off I'm in the flow of writing and continue to write beyond the time. Knowing that I only have to produce for a certain amount of time makes me feel less pressure and makes it easier to start."

— **Domenica Favero, Associate Professor of Psychological Science, author of *Introduction to Theories of Personality***

Docfy – Smart Document Scanner. "This scanning program allows you to easily scan documents and articles with your cell phone to save for later. The scanned document saves as a PDF and allows you to take notes, keep organized using folders and subfolders, and easily search either by content or keywords." [https://www.smartdocscanner.com]

— **Kathleen P. King has published more than 32 books including *147 Practical Tips for Emerging Scholars* and *The Professor's Guide to Taming Technology***

DocuSign. "This program makes signing all of those publisher authorization forms much faster. You can sign on your phone or tablet and send it back almost immediately after receiving it." [https://go.docusign.com]

— Kathleen P. King has published more than 32 books including *147 Practical Tips for Emerging Scholars* and *The Professor's Guide to Taming Technology*

DropBox. "My coauthor and I use this document sharing platform to access the document at specific times of day. My coauthor generally writes in the afternoon while I have the early day slot. Dropbox also alerts the other person when changes have been made thus keeping us engaged and feeling sufficiently "guilty" that we have not contributed yet or have ignored the task for a few days due to more important responsibility. This public notice of contribution helps each of us reengage with the work to be done and also keeps us informed of what the other has done." [https://www.dropbox.com]

— Joanna Salapska-Gelleri, Associate Professor of Cognitive Psychology, Florida Gulf Coast University, and co-author of *Mind, Brain, and Artificial Intelligence*

Focus Booster. "This app can be used online or mobile. It uses the Pomodoro Technique. You create a list of what you want to get accomplished. As you do your work, it tracks your productivity daily and weekly so you can see where you need to improve." [https://www.focusboosterapp.com]]

— Gladys Childs, Dean of Freshman Success, author of articles and the forthcoming *Logic Made Easy*, published by Cognella

Focus Keeper. "This iOS app allows you to break up the workflow into 25-minute segments with 5-minute breaks in between. You can skip the breaks if you choose to, but the app helps the user to approach a project in bite-size pieces."

— Katya Jordan, Assistant Professor of Russian

Focus at Will. "Using this app is my auditory cue that it is time to write. I use a different play list for writing vs. other work. It keeps me focused, knowing that once my time frame for writing is ended, the music will end." [https://www.focusatwill.com]

— Dana C. Kemery, Associate Professor College of Nursing and Health Professions, Drexel University

Forest. "This app incentivizes you for not using your phone. You set it for a period of time, and it rewards you for not using your phone by growing you a digital tree from a sapling to a forest depending on how long you remain away from your phone." [https://www.forestapp.cc]

— Burcu Izci, Assistant Professor, Early Childhood Education

Google Sheets. "I use Google Sheets to record the date, the daily goal (in hours/minutes), how many hours I actually worked that day, and what I worked on. This helps me to keep track of my weekly time goals and lets me know where to start each day."

— Lisa Daniels, Professor of Economics and International Studies, Washington College

Microsoft Teams. "This is a great program as it allows you to create just that, teams of collaborators, and add documents that are stable and stick around the system, so you can go back to past teams and meetings and retrieve them. You can also audio/video record your meetings. This has proven very helpful when talking to an editor at latter stages of manuscript development so you can record the meeting, with their permission, and have the conversations and suggestions of the editor handy when you review your notes, meeting, and their suggestions and guidance." [https://www.microsoft.com/en-us/microsoft-365/microsoft-teams/group-chat-software]

— Joanna Salapska-Gelleri, Associate Professor of Cognitive Psychology, Florida Gulf Coast University, and co-author of *Mind, Brain, and Artificial Intelligence*

OneNote. "I use OneNote religiously. I have notebooks for every area of my life and work. Each notebook is divided into sections and filled with pages of resources, links, and more. The biggest benefit of OneNote is that I can start on any device and pick up where I left off on any other device so there's no need to recreate something when I get to my computer – I just open it in OneNote." [https://www.onenote.com]

— Eric Schmieder, textbook author and college faculty member, computer technology discipline

Passion Planner. "This tool's goal is to help people plan for success by guiding them through a process to determine what is most important to them and then how to schedule time every day to meet goals. Writing to publish is important to researchers, so it becomes a priority for daily planning and time management." [https://passionplanner.com]

— Teresa Bell, Association Professor of German and Second Language Acquisition

Prolifiko. "This productivity coaching service offers a unique time management program for writing with a blend of webinars and a goal setting calendar where writing goals are met with gold stars once completed. It is specifically designed for writing productivity and works better than word or page counts because it is writing goal oriented." [https://prolifiko.com]

— Christine Tulley, Professor of English, author of *How Writing Faculty Write*, and Defend and Publish Coach

RescueTime. "This free app is a lifesaver. It tracks how I spend time on my computer and categorizes the time into productive and nonproductive activities. Each week, I receive a report that shows how I spent my computer time. When my writing time is too low compared to activities like email, I can adjust my plan for the coming week." [https://www.rescuetime.com]

— Tracy Tuten, author of *Principles of Marketing for a Digital Age*

Stickk. "This software helps you set short-term and long-term goals, creates an analysis sheet, and displays graphs to show your performance. It also sends you day-to-day reminders, basically acting as a focus coach." [https://www.stickk.com]

— Thrishika Potan, CIE graduate student at Loyola Academy, author of published nutrition-based journal article, writer and content creator

TextExpander. "This software tool allows you to keep a huge, organized file of short or long snippets of text and instantly add them to your project as you write. For example, you can program the abbreviation ";aud" to insert a two-sentence tip into your book reminding readers of the audio chapter summary that is available at the book website." [https://textexpander.com]

— Kevin Patton, author of award-winning textbooks and manuals in human anatomy and physiology

The Most Dangerous Writing App. "This app asks you to set a writing time goal and then locks your phone during that time. To ensure you keep writing, it sends you notifications whenever you stop or close the app before completing your time goal." [https://www.squibler.io/dangerous-writing-prompt-app]

— Thrishika Potan, CIE graduate student at Loyola Academy, author of published nutrition-based journal article, writer and content creator

TimeStory. "This is an excellent and easy Mac app for illustrating events on a timeline. It's also simple to use, scalable up to large projects, designed to help you produce a professional, attractive output." [https://timestory.app]

— Ahmed Ibrahim, PhD, Sr. Education Research Consultant, Johns Hopkins University

Trello. "This tool is very useful for managing writing projects because it enables you to break everything down into small, do-able steps. Even with the free version, there are a lot of options and versatility. Trello also provides numerous templates, which you can modify for your specific project. Whether it is writing a journal article or working on a book manuscript, Trello is a great way to get organized and stay on task." [https://trello.com]

— Margaret Puskar-Pasewicz, academic editor, indexer, and writing coach

Wunderlist. "This powerful to-do app allows you to share lists with coauthors, print your lists, schedule email reminders and other notifications, and sync across all of your devices." [https://www.wunderlist.com]

— Kathleen P. King has published more than 32 books including *147 Practical Tips for Emerging Scholars* and *The Professor's Guide to Taming Technology*

Zoom. "This is handy for conference meetings. You can also record the event and play it back later. Recording is also helpful when you want to share the progress or discussion you had with a member, team, or editor if one of the group is not available to be at the meeting." [https://zoom.us]

— Joanna Salapska-Gelleri, Associate Professor of Cognitive Psychology, Florida Gulf Coast University, and co-author of *Mind, Brain, and Artificial Intelligence*

Zotero's Group Libraries. "When working with co-authors, it is much faster to share what we are reading if we use Group Libraries. We have access to the source materials and our comments about them." [https://www.zotero.org]

— Dr. Óscar Fernández, Diversity, Equity, and Inclusion Coordinator, University Studies, Portland State University

CPSIA information can be obtained
at www.ICGtesting.com
Printed in the USA
BVHW021545070920
588053BV00002B/4